Guide to the
Western Islands
of Scotland

David Perrott

Kittiwake Press in association with
John Bartholomew & Son Ltd

Published by
The Kittiwake Press in association with
John Bartholomew & Son Ltd,
Duncan Street, Edinburgh EH9 1TA

Fourth revised edition 1989.
© Text and maps: David Perrott 1989.

Photographs: David Perrott unless stated otherwise

Line drawings: Pamela Dowson

Special thanks to Eric Jones

Typesetting and origination: Litho Link, Welshpool, Powys

Printing and binding: Richard Clay, The Chaucer Press,
Bungay, Suffolk, England

Front cover: The island of Coll. *Scottish Tourist Board.*

ISBN 0 7028 0886 5

4/5.0/4.89

Introduction

The Western Islands of Scotland are a very remote and beautiful part of Europe, with their own history, their own unique way of life and, especially in the Outer Hebrides, their own language. A visit will be much more rewarding if you are well briefed before you go and well guided when you are there. This book has been produced to satisfy both these needs.

Each island is mapped to familiarise the traveller with the lie of the land (dark shading indicates the 1000 ft contour), with the text setting the scene historically and continuing to describe all the places of interest, as if on a guided tour. Photographs and line drawings give a visual impression, and all ferry services are detailed.

The content is arranged geographically, in order that you may identify other islands in the vicinity and learn about those as well. To locate any specific island quickly, the index should be used.

When you go, bear in mind that the weather, whilst generally mild, can be extremely changeable – calm, sunny and warm one day, a force eight gale the next – so pack accordingly. In August expect to be harassed by midges. At all times respect the lifestyle of the indigenous population, and care for the wildlife and countryside.

Order of content

The Western Islands of Scotland

The Outer Hebrides

Western Isles. With an area of 716,000 acres and a population of 30,900, this is an archipelago 130 miles long, lying in a crescent about 40 miles off the north-west mainland of Scotland. The west coast is pounded by the unbroken force of the North Atlantic. The name Hebrides is derived from the Norse *Havbredey*, the 'isles on the edge of the sea'. They consist mainly of Lewisian gneiss, said to be the oldest known fragment of Europe. Of the 200-plus islands in the group, only 13 are now inhabited, with about 80 per cent of the population living on Lewis and Harris.

Of the many physical aspects setting the islands apart from the rest of Scotland perhaps the most memorable is the quality of the light. Reflected off the clear water of the surrounding sea it accentuates edges and heightens colours with its luminosity. Other times the dark storm clouds come in procession from the west, or the sea mist envelops everything. The climate is mild, with no extremes of temperature or rainfall but the wind blows strongly two days in three, especially in the north.

Most visitors to the Outer Hebrides approach from the east. The first impression is that of a barren, rock-strewn land, broken by flooded glaciated valleys, narrow and steep sided. But if the approach were from the west, the first sight would be of long white beaches, backed with fertile grassland grazed by cattle and dotted with cottages. Between these two contrasting coasts lies peat moor and a landscape which, although appearing devoid of trees, has most types present. Over 800 plant species have been recorded on the islands.

There are many prehistoric stone structures throughout the islands, the most famous being the stone circles at Callanish, built about 4000 years ago when the climate was drier and warmer, and the inhospitable peat bogs were less extensive.

The patterns of human population are very different between the northern and southern islands. Harris and the Isle of Lewis (together with Barra) reached their zenith in 1911 (35,000 people) due to the quite exceptional circumstances surrounding the herring fisheries. The pattern of North and South Uist is more comparable with that of the rest of the islands of Scotland, reaching over 14,000 in 1841, then succumbing to the clearances. Much land is still held by absentee landlords, being left fallow for sporting activities.

Today the Outer Hebrides is the last major stronghold of the Gaelic language, due probably to the physical distance of the islands from the mainland. In the Outer Hebrides a life-style and culture have survived that elsewhere have virtually disappeared. Gaelic, once the subject of derision on the mainland, is now actively promoted in the Outer Hebrides in the face of the insidious influence of television.

Lewis, Harris and North Uist are Protestant, South Uist and Barra are Roman Catholic, and Benbecula is a mixture of the two. There is no friction between the two religious communities – in fact the geography of the Sound of Harris has caused North Uist to have more contact with its Roman Catholic neighbours than with Lewis and Harris.

The main body of Protestants belong to the Free Presbyterian Church, with its strict observance of the Sabbath; Stornoway on Lewis is a major stronghold of the Lord's Day Observance Society. On Sunday, on the Protestant islands, all the bars, restaurants and shops close (making it difficult for those in bed-and-breakfast accommodation), public transport ceases and people go out only to attend church services, during which no hymns are sung. Sundays on South Uist and Barra are a more lively affair.

The *traditional* form of entertainment is still the ceilidh, originally meaning gossiping house but more recently a gathering with music.

The Outer Hebrides appeal to visitors as a perfect place to get away from it all. There is a Hebridean saying that reflects the atmosphere of these islands: 'When God made time, he made plenty of it.' The people are friendly and helpful towards tourists, but they have done little to provide organised facilities. There is no need. Nature endowed them with lochs full of salmon and trout and sea fishing of equal quality. It provided rugged scenery under wide open skies. The west coast has beaches the equal of any in Europe, deserted even on warm days. The seas are clear and clean, but, naturally, a little cold. Archaeologists will find some of the finest sites in the country, and ornithologists can seek out rare and unique species. As part of its policy of preserving the Gaelic language, the Western Isles Islands Council has installed Gaelic road signs throughout the islands. A leaflet is available from the local Tourist Information Centres giving the English equivalents – make sure you obtain a copy on arrival.

Isle of Lewis

The name derived from *leogach* (pronounced loo-ach) meaning marshy. The largest and most populous island in the Outer Hebrides, with 21,540 inhabitants, it borders Harris to the north of the Forest of Harris, a natural barrier of wild moorland and mountain. The island is made up almost wholly of gneiss, rising to 1885 ft at the summit of Mealisval in the south-west, and to 1874 ft at the summit of Beinn Mhór in the south. Much of the gneiss is overlaid with glacially deposited boulder clay. There are small areas of Torridonian sandstone near Stornoway and several hundred acres of granite in the parish of Barvas.

The dominant feature of Lewis is the dark, undulating central peat moor, scattered with hundreds of shallow lochs. Although its appearance is uniform, its sheer size is impressive. Centuries of peat cutting have enlivened the surface of the moor with circles, squares and snaking lines, each cut having a herring-bone pattern. The cutting takes place in the early summer, when the moor becomes alive with families engaged in this work. Later, when the cut peat has dried, it is carried away from the banks in sacks, barrows, car boots and modified tractors and trailers to be used as fuel. Going to the peats is very much a social occasion.

The peat began to form about 7000 years ago. Under generally cold, wet and acidic conditions the growth of sedge, moss, grass and heather outstrips the rate at which the dead plants decompose and the layer of peat – fibrous plant remains – begins to thicken. Lewis peat is a mixture of sphagnum and deergrass which, on some parts of the moor, is still making. The peat in the deeper, blacker layers is a fine fuel, clean and easy to handle when dry, but its calorific value is only two-thirds that of coal. In its natural state the water content can be as high as 90 per cent. The reserves of peat on Lewis have been estimated at 85 million tons, and it is still cut in the traditional way. A good worker, with helpers, can cut 1000 peats a day, which then have to be drained, dried and transported. A crofting family would use around 15,000 each year. The neatly stacked peats – the *cruach* – by the crofts and houses represent a large investment of time and labour and the islanders are justly proud of them.

The main pillars of the Lewis economy are weaving, fishing, crofting (there are about 3500 small crofts, generally worked on a part-time basis), and to some extent tourism. This variety has brought a measure of stability lacking on other islands with less diverse sources of income. If a cold wind blows in one sector of the Lewis economy, such as the short-lived oil rig construction industry, there are others to fall back on.

Known worldwide is Harris tweed and the centre of production is Lewis. Harris tweed can only be sold as such if it is made in the Outer Hebrides from virgin Scottish wool, woven on hand-looms in the weavers' own homes. It must also bear the orb trademark of the Harris Tweed Association, founded in 1909. The hard-wearing, warm and water-resistant cloth is produced 28½ inches wide, in rolls of 38 weaver's yards (each being 72 inches). The tweed was originally produced for the crofters' own use until its wider applications were promoted by the wives of the landowners, such as

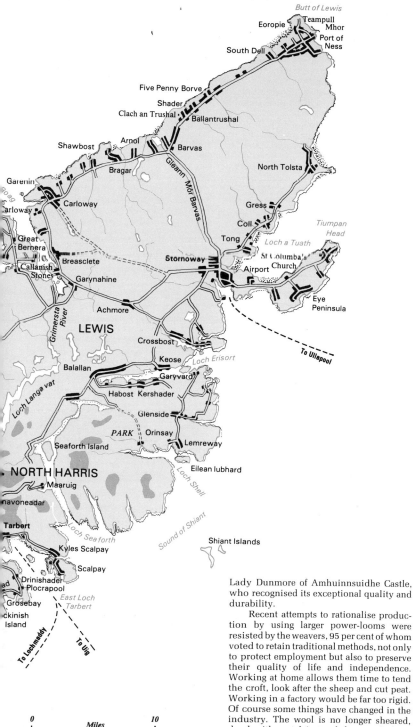

Lady Dunmore of Amhuinnsuidhe Castle, who recognised its exceptional quality and durability.

Recent attempts to rationalise production by using larger power-looms were resisted by the weavers, 95 per cent of whom voted to retain traditional methods, not only to protect employment but also to preserve their quality of life and independence. Working at home allows them time to tend the croft, look after the sheep and cut peat. Working in a factory would be far too rigid. Of course some things have changed in the industry. The wool is no longer sheared, dyed with crotal (natural dyes made from lichen) over a peat fire, carded and spun at the croft – all this has been done in the factory at Stornoway since 1934. The prepared wool is delivered to the weaver, and the finished cloth collected by van from the factory. The finished bundles of tweed can be seen lying at the roadside, in all sorts of weather, awaiting collection. The only tweed produced by entirely traditional methods is made by Marion Campbell of Plocrapool, who spins, dyes and weaves in the original way.

The hand-looms are usually housed in small sheds; a rhythmic clacking reveals work in progress. The weaver sits at the loom, his legs providing the power and his hands changing the shuttles. It looks, and is, hard work. There are 650 such weavers on Lewis and Harris producing some 4½ million yards, the skill traditionally being passed down the generations, although it can now be learned at the technical college in Stornoway.

The first owners of Lewis were clans of Norse origin. Later, the island became part of Scotland, with the MacLeods being replaced by the Mackenzies of Kintail in 1610, who then held the island until 1844 when Mrs Stewart Mackenzie sold it to Sir James Matheson for £190,000. He invested £500,000 (earned from the China trade) on improvements – draining land, building schools and financing industries.

Lord Leverhulme bought the island (along with Harris) in 1918, intending to develop the fishing industry. After spending £875,000 he gave up in 1923. On leaving, he gifted the 64,000-acre parish of Stornoway to the people, to be administered by the elected Stornoway Trust, and offered crofts as free gifts, although only 41 were accepted. Much of the remaining land fell into the hands of speculators and absentee landlords. The slump resulting from his withdrawal caused the emigration of over 1000 able-bodied men to North America, some of whom returned during the Depression of the 1930s.

In the heyday of the herring fishing industry over 1000 boats operated from Stornoway, but the loss of men during World War I and Norwegian competition brought about its eventual demise. The white-fish industry suffered from steam trawlers fishing illegally and destroying the local line-fishing gear. Now, with the aid of loans and grants, the industry is on its feet again with local boats landing white fish and prawns.

The only town of burgh status in the Hebrides, and the only town in the Outer Hebrides, is Stornoway. It is the administrative centre of the Western Isles Authority and has a steadily rising population as a result of migration from the surrounding countryside. On its outskirts there is much new housing to accommodate this influx.

The town has a fresh, cosmopolitan atmosphere, and offers a range of shops, hotels, bars, restaurants and services unique in the Western Isles. It even has a small Pakistani community – shopkeepers with a working knowledge of Gaelic.

The fine natural harbour provides shelter in all conditions, and is host to local and visiting fishing boats and traders as well as the Caledonian MacBrayne vehicle ferry *Suilven* from Ullapool. The lifeboat based here is responsible for one of the largest areas in the British Isles. A colony of grey seals has also made its home in the harbour. The oil industry construction yard, now disused, is situated at Arnish Point. On **Eilean na Gobhail** (goat island) opposite, there are ship-repair facilities and a slipway. To the north of the harbour are the Beasts of Holm. It was on these rocks, at 1.55 on the morning of 1 January 1919 that the steamer *Iolaire*, ferrying Lewis men from the Kyle of Lochalsh on the final leg of their journey home from the war, was wrecked. 205 of the 285 on board drowned. Rumours of drunkeness among the crew were rife in the islands until the public enquiry, held in Stornoway the following month, found no evidence whatsoever to support this view. The Tourist Information Centre is situated in South Beach Street.

Lews Castle

The 18thC net-loft on North Beach Quay is probably the oldest buiding still standing in the town. St Peter's Episcopal Church has the prayer book taken by David Livingstone on his travels. Martin's Memorial, the spired church in Francis Street, was built in the 19thC at the birthplace of Sir Alexander Mackenzie, the man who made the first overland crossing of Canada. The police headquarters, the Sheriff Court and two hospitals are also situated in the town, along with the Nicholson Institute, a senior comprehensive school founded in 1873 by a Lewisman subsequently killed in Shanghai. There is a sports centre and swimming pool, a golf course and a cinema. The sea fishing in this area is excellent and boat trips are arranged by the local sea-angling club.

To the west of the town is the turreted Lews Castle, built by Sir James Matheson during the 1840s, and surrounded by a square mile of beautiful mixed woodland. These woods, unique in the Outer Hebrides, have been colonised by a wide variety of woodland birds and there is also a large rookery of about 150 nests. What were once private gardens are planted with berberis, azalea, fuchsia and rhododendron. The Stornoway Trust now uses the castle as a technical college, where navigation, weaving, building and engineering are taught.

To the east of Stornoway is the comparatively densely populated Eye Peninsula, known as Point. Stornoway airport, to the north of the road to Point, is both civil and military, being used as Nato base.

At the very western end of Point by the north shore stand the walls of the now defunct 14thC St Columba's Church and the graveyard of Ui, an important religious site said to have been built where St Catan had his cell in the 7thC. The graveyard is the burial ground of 19 MacLeod chiefs of Lewis. There is a fine effigy of Roderick MacLeod on the south side of the church and an impressive Celtic stone on the north. The last service was held here in 1828. The rest of the peninsula is of little interest, being undulating moorland shared by crofters and commuters. There are pleasant small beaches near Bayble and Garrabost, and a lighthouse at Tiumpan Head.

North-east of Stornoway the road passes the beaches at Coll and Gress, before ending near Tolsta by Tràigh Mhór, a fine sweep of dune-backed sands with caves and stacks nearby. The road to Tolsta was built by Lord Leverhulme, who intended it to become part of a circuit of northern Lewis, connecting with the Port of Ness. North of Tolsta, the coast is inaccessible by car, remaining isolated, lonely and wild.

The road from Stornoway to Barvas crosses the central peat moor, following the north-west course of the River Barvas (a salmon river) until it meets the west coast road. This road, with its scattered crofting/weaving townships, follows a route about a mile inland, and little of interest can be seen without leaving it.

The first impression given by the townships is one of untidyness – old houses are left to crumble while new ones remain not quite finished. Cars stand abandoned right outside front doors, although it must be said that the interiors of the houses are given a great deal of attention and care. What we see has two explanations. The communities are virtually classless and non-competitive in the modern urban sense so there is no desire to impress the neighbours with outside appearances. Sec-

ondly, while the people do wish to have new houses, cars, etc., they seem not to want to make a clear break with the past, so old things that have served them well are left to just fade away.

It was from the townships of Barvas that the idea of re-seeding the barren moorland spread. Initially the surface of the moor is skimmed, after which lime-rich shell sand, nitrous phosphate and fertiliser are spread, seeds are sown, and worms and bacteria turn the whole lot into soil. Many thousands of acres have been improved in this way under the Crofters Commission Land Improvement Scheme. It raises the grazing potential for sheep 30-fold and, where the reclaimed land adjoins the moorland, the contrast is quite dramatic. In March 1980 Barvas was the scene of a unique referendum to see whether the people wished to have licensed premises in the parish. The idea was defeated by two to one and drinking continues in *bothans*, shacks on common ground, tolerated by the police. Strangers are *not* welcome.

The tallest standing stone in the Hebrides, Clach an Trushal, stands overlooking the sea at Ballantrushal. To the east of Loch an Dùin at Shader is Steinacleit, a 50-ft diameter burial cairn encircled by stones, in a large oval enclosure. It stands on the skyline and can be reached via a rough track. From Dell to Port of Ness there are many crofts and the land is green and sandy. On the coast, between Dell and Eoropie, are several small sandy bays, from which the natural arch at Roinn a' Roidh can be seen. Just beyond the arch is **Luchruban**, the tidal 'pigmy's isle'. Its claim to occupation by small people is unfounded, as the bones found here were more likely the remains of food consumed by the occupant of an ancient stone cell, the remnants of which can still be seen. It is from the small harbour at Port of Ness that the men of the district leave every August to bring back guga (young gannet), considered quite a delicacy, from Sula Sgeir, 41 miles to the north.

The most northerly village in the Outer Hebrides is Eoropie. The key to the restored 12thC Church of St Moluag (Teampull Mholuidh) in a field to the north can be obtained from the store.

The red-brick lighthouse and white foghorn tower at the Butt of Lewis stand above the rocky northern tip of the island. 44 miles north-north-east is the tiny island of Rona (North Rona), and 200 miles north are the Faeroes. To the south-east of the Butt is the attractive tiny Port Sto.

Heading south-west from Barvas the road passes Loch Mór Barvas, a refuge for wildfowl, before reaching Arnol. At the far end of the township is The Black House museum. This *tigh dubh*, last occupied in 1964, has walls six-feet thick, with a roof of

The Butt of Lewis lighthouse

thatch over turf, weighted with ropes and stones. A peat fire burns in the centre of the floor, and there is no chimney. These structures were warm, dry and quiet when the wind outside howled. Visitors see authentic room settings, including straw-lined box beds. Arnol stands at the edge of the machair (see Harris), where the crofts are divided by stone dykes. The original settlement, along with others on this western seaboard of Lewis, was closer to the sea, on a site occupied since the 1stC AD, but winter storms and the exhaustion of the peat beds resulted in re-siting during the 18thC. Nearby Loch na Muilne, a mill loch, powered several of the township's water-mills.

By the roadside at Bragar there is a whalebone arch some 20-ft high – suspended from it is the harpoon that killed the whale. The children of Shawbost, the next village, made a splendid folk museum for the 1970 Highland Village Competition which is now housed in a converted church to the south of the road.

By the coast at Carloway is the village of Garenin. At the end of the road, above a sheltered shingle bay, is the last remaining street of black houses in Lewis (in fact, some are white houses – *tigh geal* – the dry stone

walls having been cemented, and the roofs tarred). The last family left here about 1973.

Doune Carloway is a well-preserved broch with the tallest part of the wall standing over 22 ft high and a diameter of 47 ft. The galleries, staircase and entrance can be clearly seen, and the view from it is superb.

Doune Carloway

The main road now heads south along the side of East Loch Roag which is scattered with low-lying islands. Between Carloway and Breasclete the land becomes more hilly with many small lochs. Hidden by the shore is the pretty village of Tolsta Chaolais. What was once the shore station for the Flannan Isles lighthouse stands in Breasclete.

At the head of East Loch Roag is Callanish, site of a stone circle probably erected 4000 years ago, equal in importance to Stonehenge. The monoliths make a rough

Achmore, Lewis

Celtic cross 405 ft north to south, 140 ft east to west. 47 are now left, the tallest over 15 ft high, and within the central circle is a cairn where the remains of the cremation were found. It was not until 1857, when five feet of peat was dug away that the true height and extent of the stones was seen. Various theories exist regarding their true purpose – at present the astro-archaeological one seems the most credible. Professor Gerald Hawkins, an American astronomer, has used a computer to verify 12 significant astronomical alignments, one of the main ones being mid-summer moonset, south along the main avenue, over Clisham on Harris. Whereas Stonehenge seems to relate to the sun, Callanish seems to relate to the moon. There is still much more research to be done before firm conclusions can be drawn and such studies will have to include the many other smaller stone circles in the area which also align with Callanish. A local legend claims that the stones are really giants, petrified by St Kieran for refusing to be christened. The University of Edinburgh Archaeology Department now owns the adjacent Callanish Farm, using it as a study centre.

After Garynahine, the main road traverses the central moorland on its way to Stornoway, a minor road leaving it to head south-west to Great Bernera and Uig, and soon crossing the Abhainn Grimersta river, which is fed by the remote Loch Langavat and acknowledged as one of the best salmon rivers in Europe. To the north is the hilly and loch-strewn island of **Great Bernera** in Loch Roag. It is the largest of over 40 islands in the loch, the other notable ones, all uninhabited, being **Little Bernera, Vuia Mór, Vacsay** with population of nine in 1861 and sold for £9500 in 1983, **Pabay Mór** (population of 17 in 1861) where there are the remains of a church, and **Drasay** which once had a population of two. This whole area surrounding Loch Roag is, without doubt, one of the most attractive parts of Lewis. The many freshwater lochs make good fishing for brown trout, and the mountains to the south-west are the haunt of golden eagles, peregrine falcons and buzzards. Great Bernera is a lobster-fishing centre and, in 1972, a fish-processing plant was built at Kirkibost on the east side. The name most common on the island is MacDonald, said to be descendants of a watchman who was given the island as reward for his services to the MacAulays of Uig. The bridge was opened in 1953 after the islanders threatened to construct a causeway themselves by dynamiting the cliffs. There is a small sheltered beach, facing Little Bernera, beyond the deserted village of Bosta. To the north-west is the island of **Bearasay**, retreat of Neil MacLeod, who defeated the Fife Adventurers (merchants who tried to take over the island in the 16thC to exploit the herring fishing), but who later turned pirate and was eventually executed.

To reach Uig the road passes round Little Loch Roag through typical peat and rock scenery. At Carishader, on the west shore of Loch Roag, the scenery again becomes attractive. Behind Miavaig the road passes through the lovely steep-sided green and rocky Glen Valtos – an atypical sight on Lewis and a nice surprise. A minor road completes a circuit of Cliff, Valtos, Reef and Uigen. There are superb beaches here, especially the dune-backed shell sands of Tràigh na Berie, sheltered by Pabay Móy and Vacsay. To the north of Glen Valtos is the township of Aird Uig, and Gallan Head. The Flannan Isles are 21 miles north-west into the Atlantic.

The Uig Sands are beautiful – wide, clean, flat and well sheltered – access is good, and the grassland at the back of the beach is flat enough for a football pitch. The whole is overlooked by the cream-painted and slated Uig Lodge and the superbly sited school at Timsgarry. A hand-carved walrus-ivory chess set of Norse origin dating back to about 1150 was found in 1831 at Ardroil, by a herdsman whose beast uncovered it in the dunes. Parts of the set are now in the British and the Scottish National Museums.

The view inland from Uig, along the glen between Mealisval and Tahaval, is dramatic and a refreshing change from the peat moor of the north. The road ends at Brenish. Beyond here was Tigh nan Cailleachan Dubha (house of the black old women), a Benedictine convent possibly associated with Iona. To the south is **Mealasta Island**, lying about half a mile off the coast, where the mountains drop steeply to the sea.

To the south of Stornoway is the parish of Lochs, aptly named as, in parts, there seems to be more water than land. It is best seen early or late in the day when the water appears like mercury against the dark peat moor. The coast here is steep and rocky with no beaches, and narrow sea lochs cut deeply into the land – Loch Seaforth, for example, brings salt water some 12 miles inland.

The most rewarding areas of this parish are well off the main road. To the north of Loch Erisort lies the smaller inlet of Loch Leurbost with the villages of Leurbost, Crossbost, Ranish and Grimshader all attractively sited to the north and linked by a loop road. The seaward end of the lochs are littered with small islands.

Further south, a minor road connects with Keose and the alginate factory, where seaweed collected from around the island is processed. Alginate from here apparently went to the moon – fireproofing the astronauts' notepads. Beyond the crofting township of Balallan which straggles along the road for two-and-a-half miles, a splendid roadsign names no less than 11 villages to be found by following the route along the southern shore of Loch Erisort to Cromore, Marvig and Lemreway. The first habitations to be passed are Habost, Kershader and Garyvard, all refreshing places, with grass, conifers and rowan.

At Cromore, **Eilean Chaluim Chille**, with its ruined church dedicated to St Columba and small burial ground, can be seen. The main road finishes at Lemreway, situated at the back of a bay sheltered by **Eilean Iubhard**.

To the south of Loch Erisort and to the east of Loch Seaforth, is the treeless Park (or Pairc) deer forest, where herds of red deer roam freely. It was here, in 1887, that one of the last uprisings of the Crofters' War (which began with the Battle of the Braes on Skye) took place. The crofters, desperate for more land, killed 200 deer to draw attention to their plight – and entertained invited journalists to roast venison in order to obtain wide coverage by the press. The leaders of the Deer Raid were later tried and found not guilty of mobbing and rioting. The 57,000 acre estate is still privately owned and is used for hunting, fishing and little else.

Harris

With a population of 2140, Harris is separated from Lewis by the deep incisions of Loch Seaforth and Loch Resort, and six miles of mountainous and treeless deer forest rising to a height of 2622 ft at the summit of Clisham, the highest point in the Outer Hebrides. North Harris is separated from South Harris by the narrow neck of land at Tarbert, where two sea lochs almost cut the island in two.

Gneiss, the rock of the Outer Hebrides, is nowhere more apparent than on Harris, always visible even if covered here and there with peat or water or strewn with boulders. It is only on the west coast that a narrow border of machair brings some relief. Machair is the low-lying, sometimes undulating, land behind the dunes and the stabilising fringe of marram grass. It consists of as many as 50 types of flowering plants among grass, growing on wind-blown shell sand. Its fertility is enhanced by animal dung and the spreading of seaweed manure. It is easily damaged by overgrazing and the erosive effects of rabbits and of wheeled vehicles.

Hushinish, Harris

Untilled, the soil forms a layer about six inches thick, uniform and free from stones. With cultivation and the addition of seaweed it often reaches a depth of 12 inches. The wind is constantly spreading fresh shell sand over the machair – a natural dressing of lime. On these gneiss islands, the fertile machair is a vital land resource. In early summer, when in flower it is brilliantly coloured and is so heady with perfume that it is said it can flavour the milk of grazing dairy cattle. Against the blue sea and the white shell-sand beaches, it is magical.

The people of Harris, although said to have the same Norse ancestry as Lewis, have a different dialect, with fewer words of Norse derivation and spoken with a softer lilt. The island was held by the MacLeods of Harris from the time of the Norse surrender in the 13thC until 1779, when it was sold to Captain Macleod of Berneray who invested in a fishing industry for the island building the harbour at Rodel and numerous roads, as well as restoring Rodel church and planting many trees. The Earl of Dunmore purchased Harris in 1834, later selling the north to Sir Edward Scott in 1868 and the south to Lord Leverhulme in 1919. After the latter's scheme to revitalise the island and its fishing industry failed, in 1923 much of the land was sold to absentee landlords who sold off assets, built by Lord Leverhulme, with scant regard for the indigenous population. Eventually some of the land that was cleared in the 19thC was purchased by the Government and returned to the crofters.

Before the Clearances the population had risen far beyond that which the land could reasonably support and living standards were intolerably low. Such were the pressures that lazybeds, strips of fertile soil built by hand on top of the rock and used for growing potatoes and oats, were stretching 500 ft up the hillsides in places. In the 19thC depopulation was seen as the only possible way of raising living standards.

The main occupations today are crofting, weaving (Harris tweed originated here but the centre of production is now Lewis), knitting, fishing and little else. As a result, depopulation continues steadily, with many young people leaving to find employment elsewhere.

Tarbert is the largest village. There are a few shops, some selling knitwear and tweed, a post office, hotel and ferry terminal. The Caledonian MacBrayne ferry *Hebridean Isles* links with Uig and

Skye and Lochmaddy on North Uist. A small Tourist Information Centre is open during the summer, and there is hostel accommodation at Kyles Stockinish (SYHA) and Rhenigidale (Gatliff Trust).

North Harris

East Loch Tarbert is littered with many rocks and islands, the largest of which are **Scotasay** which had a population of 20 in 1911 but is now deserted, and the thriving Scalpay, reached via the ferry from Kyles Scalpay. The road to the ferry winds along the north side of the loch, past crofts forged out of the barren ground. Many now have well-tended gardens – in one, two small palm trees grow! A path from Urgha leads north along Laxadale Lochs to Maaruig on Loch Seaforth.

To the north of West Loch Tarbert are the high bare mountains of the Forest of Harris. On the shore, beneath Clisham, is Bunavoneadar where there are the remains of a whaling station built by Norwegians about 1912. It was utilised by Lord Leverhulme as part of his revitalisation scheme, being finally abandoned in 1930.

The narrow road winds around the head of Loch Meavaig, where the view north along the glen, between the steep and craggy sides of Oreval (2172 ft) and Sròn Scourst (1611 ft), is quite dramatic. In a beautiful and isolated position above the township of Meavaig stands the corrugated-iron school, neat, tidy and painted cream. Here the children learn and play looking out towards **Soay Beag, Soay Mór** and Taransay, a fine prospect.

Beyond Cliasmol, with its maze of lazybeds, is the baronial-style Amhuinnsuidhe Castle (pronounced Ah-vin-soo-ee), standing by the pretty inlet of Loch Leosavay. Built by the Earl of Dunmore in 1868, the castle is of attractive warm-grey stone imported into Harris. The road approaches the castle through white gates and passes the falls where the waters of Loch Leosaid tumble into the sea. Here, in June and July, salmon can be seen leaping. The west entrance to the grounds is through a fine archway, beyond which there is a sturdy terrace of stone houses and stables.

The castle gardens are planted with shrubs and lilies, and pheasants wander among the trees. It was at Amhuinnsuidhe Castle in 1912 that James Barrie, the Scottish author and dramatist, conceived of the drama *Mary Rose*, inspired, it is said, by one of the small islets in Loch Voshimid, four-and-a-half miles to the north-east.

Most of this part of Harris, including the castle, is privately owned. The herds of red deer that roam the hills are carefully protected, the lochs are rich with salmon and trout, and golden eagles and ravens haunt the peaks. The castle is available for weekly lets to those who can afford it.

A mile inland from Amhuinnsuidhe, Loch Chliostair feeds a new hydroelectric power station which supplies most of Harris. The arch dam built here was the first of its type in the Outer Hebrides. The road continues north-west through an area of peat before reaching the small crofting community of Hushinish. To the west of the superb beach, low cliffs of rose-coloured gneiss shelter guillemots, shags and fulmars. Cattle and sheep graze behind the dunes. When a strong southerly wind blows, the sands spread everywhere, sometimes burying the road. A short distance to the north a small pier serves the island of **Scarp**, first settled around 1810, but abandoned by its last remaining crofters in 1971. In the 1940s the population was still over 100, but the cottages are now used as holiday homes. This rocky island rises to a height of 1011 ft in the north; the 'village' is sheltered from the prevailing winds by a smaller hill in the east of the island. In 1934, well before the army brought its missiles to South Uist, an experiment was conducted here by Gerhard Zucha to see if mail could be sent to and from Scarp by rocket. On the first firing, celebrated with a special stamp issue, the projectile exploded on impact and most of the mail was damaged. The service ceased. Sold recently for £80,000, there are now plans to develop a luxury holiday complex on Scarp. Several small islands lie offshore. Five miles to the south-west is the low-lying islet of **Gasker**, which has a seal colony.

Amhuinnsuidhe Castle, Harris

The Church of St Clement, Rodel

South Harris

The eastern coastline, known as Bays, is broken with narrow sea lochs and many small islands; inland the gneiss is spattered with hundreds of small lochs. The coast road (or Golden Road, so called because it was so expensive to build) winds through this dramatic heather-clad and rock-strewn landscape where boulders balance precariously on hill slopes and small dwellings nestle in dips and hollows.

Many crofters came here when the fertile land in the west was cleared for sheep, having to grow their food where none had grown before. They collected seaweed and mixed it with peat, arranging the whole in raised beds for drainage. The mixture weathered into compost and, on these lazybeds, oats and potatoes were grown. Gradually the beds were enlarged, running far up the hillsides in places, and the seaweed had to be carried further and further. A few sheep were grazed among the rocks. In the crofters' favour was the broken coastline which provided shelter for their boats and enabled them to catch herring and lobster, and the freshwater lochs which supplied trout.

But life was never easy, and neither was death. So intractable is the ground that the dead had to be taken to the west coast for burial. Here we are privileged to see a land where men and women have literally forged their existence on bare inhospital rock and the sight is an inspiration. Now that life is a little easier, there is time to grow a few flowers by the croft – an enjoyable sight among these bare hills.

At Drinishader, to the west of East Loch Tarbert, Mrs Alex MacDonald wove tweed that was presented to the Queen, Elizabeth II. Beyond Grosebay is Kyles Stockinish where a youth hostel overlooks **Stockinish Island**. The small inlet on the island is used as a lobster pond.

From Loch Flodabay the Shiant Isles can be seen 18 miles to the north-east, their tall cliffs rising steeply from the sea. After Loch Finsbay the road rises around the foot of Roineabhal (1506 ft) from which the whole panorama of the coast and the lochs can be seen.

The village of Rodel, one mile north of Renish Point, has a small harbour built in the late 16thC by Captain Macleod, sheltered by the island of Vallay and overlooked by the famous St Clement's Church, the plan of which is cruciform, with a square central tower, making it unique in the outer isles. It was built in about 1500 by Alasdair Crotach, 8th MacLeod of Dunvegan in Skye, using mellow green sandstone, some imported from Mull. His effigy, sculpted in 1528, lies in a fine arched recess tomb, beautifully and simply carved. The church has been twice restored, in 1787 and 1873. The key is available from the nearby hotel.

Two-and-a-half miles north-west of Rodel, through Gleann Shranndabhal is Leverburgh, formerly Obbe. The name was changed when Lord Leverhulme tried to revolutionise the fishing industry here. He chose Obbe, on the Sound of Harris, because it gave equal access to both the waters of the Atlantic and the Minch, so that his boats could always find sheltered water in which to fish. He planned to blast away many of the rocks and skerries that make the waters of the sound so treacherous, and he built factories and houses for his workers. The initial catches of herring exceeded expectation but the project never really worked well. He sold out in 1923, and within two years all activity had stopped. Leverburgh looks, sadly, like a failed dream, untidy and down at the heel. A small passenger ferry crosses the sound to Berneray and Newtonferry on North Uist.

At the eastern end of the South of Harris are the small green islands of **Gilsay, Lingay, Scaravay** and **Groay**. The two largest islands in the Sound are **Killegray** which once had a population of five, and **Ensay**, which once supported 15 people. Both have houses still standing, and attractive beaches. On Ensay there is a private Episcopal chapel by the house, with a fine oak door carved by Robert Thompson of Kilburn in North Yorkshire, and Viking relics have been uncovered. In summer they are grazed by sheep, and visited occasionally by the holidaying Royal Family.

After Leverburgh, the road passes through Glen Coishletter. As the summit is reached acres of glorious cream shell sand come into view, sheltered by the great bulk of Chaipaval to the west, rising to 1201 ft. It is an extremely pleasant walk through the crofting land and up to the top. The view is splendid – on a clear day St Kilda can be seen some 45 miles to the west and the Skye Cuillins 50 miles south-east. The small island of **Coppay**, which has a seal colony, can be seen one-and-a-half miles to the west. The Scarista Hotel, opened in 1978, offers fresh food and comfortable accommodation.

The road along the west coast crosses the machair behind the beaches. The crofts look prosperous, with sheep and cattle grazing nearby. The beach at Borve is excellent; at its southern end there is a standing stone. Standing in a hollow sheltered by woods planted by the Earl of Dunmore, Borve Lodge was occupied by Lord Leverhulme during his time on the island. A mile offshore is the handsome island of **Taransay** – two large humps joined by a narrow neck of dunes – where cattle and sheep can be seen grazing by the shore. Its settlement of Piable once had a population of 76, which gradually dwindled until the last family left in 1942, although it was later re-inhabited and once again abandoned in 1974. The school, by the landing, closed in 1935. Taransay once had two chapels, one dedicated to St Taran, where women were buried, the other to St Keith, where men were interred. It is said that a mixed burial in one of the grave yards resulted in a body being found on the surface the following morning. In the south west is Aird Vanish, a lonely place with sea caves and a wild storm beach.

There are more fine creamy shell sands at Tràigh Seilebost, backed by a spit of dunes, which in turn are backed by the estuarine sands of Tràigh Luskentyre. On the northern shore, behind the dunes, is the township of Luskentyre.

The road skirts the southern side of the estuary, passing saltings and then crossing a causeway before climbing between the South Harris Forest and the wild hills to the south. The view back towards Taransay is magnificent, especially in summer when the sea thrift is in bloom.

South Harris is an area of stark contrasts and is worthy of much exploration. There are fine rough walks along the harsh eastern seaboard and through the central hills and lochs. In summer, if the wind drops and the sun shines, the beaches on the west, backed by the machair in flower, are perfect for a day by the sea. The whole is unspoiled, undeveloped and uncrowded.

Scalpay

Situated off Harris at the mouth of East Loch Tarbert, Scalpay has a population of about 450 and the main industry is fishing – once for herring, but now for prawns. All the habitations are on the western seaboard and the pressure of so many people on the land resulted in extensive lazybed cultivation although most are now unused. A fine natural harbour is situated in the north-west with another on the west. On **Eilean Glas**, in the far south-east, there has been a lighthouse since 1788 – the first in the Western Isles but now superseded by a 19thC light which is now automatic. The original keep-

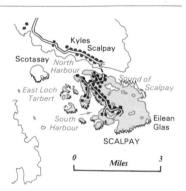

ers houses, built of Aberdeen granite by Robert Louis Stevenson's grandfather, are now let to holiday visitors.

The Scalpachs are a tight-knit and vigorous community with a strong attachment to their little island. Enlightened leadership and modest and timely investments in new equipment have allowed them to maintain their viability during periods of considerable change in the fishing industry. Bonnie Prince Charlie came here, on his way to Stornoway, after his defeat at Culloden in 1746. Donald Campbell, a farmer, gave him refuge and the use of his boat.

A small vehicle ferry, Caledonian MacBrayne's *Kilbrannan*, connects with Kyles Scalpay.

North Uist

With a population of 1660, and an area of 75,000 acres, this is a low-lying island, deeply incised in the east by the sea and so liberally endowed with freshwater lochs that half the area is covered by water, reflecting so much light that colours seem to glow and shimmer in the sun. Rising from this anglers' paradise are North and South Lee (860 ft and 922 ft respectively) and, further south, Eaval (1138 ft), the highest point on the island. In the north and west a few low hills give way to wide sandy bays with tidal islands, backed by tracts of machair, particularly attractive in the spring and early summer. With no high ground in the west, the prevailing winds blow unchecked.

After the period of Norse occupation, North Uist was ruled by the MacRuairidhs, followed by the MacDonalds of Sleat (Skye) whose official title was confirmed by James IV in 1495. They held the island until 1855, when it was sold to Sir John Powlett Ord who split the estate. It is now all owned by the enterprising Lord Granville, a cousin of the Queen.

In the early 19thC there were almost 5000 people living on the island, but a decline in population over the last 160 years has continued. Evictions were carried out

around 1850 under the direction of Lord MacDonald of Sleat, whose conduct as a landowner did him little credit. Police constables were brought to the island, cottages were burned and a bloody fight took place between the police and the crofters near Malaclete. The church minister was conspicuous by his absence during this time.

In recent years the economy has been fairly well balanced, with a spread of activities including crofting, fishing, the production of alginates, weaving and knitting, and bulb-growing has also been tried. A more recent venture is scallop farming. The crofts on North Uist are generally quite large, enabling them to be worked as a primary means of income, rather than on the part-time basis common elsewhere. There was once a large herring fishing fleet centred on Loch Maddy, but today the fishing industry is concerned mainly with lobsters and crabs, and is based on Grimsay. The alginate factory, opened in 1957, is at Sponish on Loch Maddy, where local collectors bring seaweed for processing. Knitwear and tweed are produced both on an individual and collective basis.

The islanders have been Protestant since the late 18thC, sharing their religion, strangely, with their more distant neighbours across the Sound of Harris rather than with the Catholics of South Uist and Barra. The different religious communities live in total harmony with each other.

The complex area of lochs in the east, salt and fresh, and the salmon, sea trout and brown trout they contain, are a major attraction to anglers. Fishing is controlled by the North Uist Estate and the Newton Estate. A good place to start enquiries is the hotel at Lochmaddy, the main village and terminal for the Caledonian MacBrayne ferry *Hebridean Isles* from Tarbert (Harris) and Uig (Skye). As well as the hotel, there are a couple of shops, a bank, post office, school and small hospital. The position of the village, which has a population around 300, at the back of Loch Maddy, is very attractive. There are two theories regarding the derivation of Maddy. One claims it is from the two dog (maddy) shaped rocks at the entrance to the loch, the other that the loch is rich in a certain kind of shellfish called maddies. The village is the natural centre for touring the island and for fishing.

By the road, to the north-west, Blashaval rises to 358 ft. On its western slope are three standing stones called Na Fir Bhreige, the false men, said to mark the graves of three spies who were buried alive. The north side of Loch Maddy is reached across a narrow neck of land, and there are fine views over the many islands in the loch towards North and South Lee. The east coast of the promontory has a few small hills, and

to the north, in the Sound of Harris, are the islands of **Sursay, Tahay, Vaccasay** and **Hermetray**. It was on the last that Charles I planned to establish a fishing station, but the outbreak of the Civil War brought the scheme to a premature end.

In Clachan Sands, to the west of the Newtonferry road, are the remains of the pre-Reformation church of St Columba and a burial ground. Just behind Port nan Long is the broch, Dùn an Sticir, last occupied in 1602 by Hugh MacDonald of Sleat (see Duntulm, Skye). The causeway to it can still be seen, but the building is now little more than a pile of stones. The easy climb to the summit of Beinn Mhór (625 ft), is well worthwhile; looking to the south-west the contrast between the loch-strewn east and the machair in the west can be clearly seen.

At the northern tip of North Uist is Newtonferry, where a vehicle ferry connects with Berneray and a passenger ferry with Leverburgh.

Of the three large islands visible from here – Berneray, Pabbay and Boreray – only the first is still inhabited. **Berneray** is three miles long, one-and-a-half miles wide and has a population of about 150 living in well-kept, white-painted houses on the eastern side. Although lying close to North Uist, it forms part of the Parish of Harris and is still privately owned. The island is green (there is no peat) with superb beaches. Prior to the 16thC it was almost connected to Pabbay, but strong tides swept the sands away. The people are crofters, lobster fishermen and knitters and support a campaigning and active community council. There is a post office and shop on the island, and a minibus service. Soon a new harbour is to be built.

Pabbay, four-and-a-half miles off North Uist, once supported a population of over 300 who produced, among other things, whisky. The island was cleared for sheep and is now run as a single farm. It rises to a height of 643 ft on the northern side, and was once known as the granary of Harris. On the southern shore is an old burial ground. A mile to the north are the small islands of **Shillay**, where grey seals breed.

Boreray, two-and-a-half miles north-west of Newtonferry, is one-and-a-half miles long by one mile wide, the highest point being 184 ft, and it has a large central loch. In 1841 it supported a population of 181, but it was evacuated by request in 1923, although one family changed its mind at the last minute, obtaining a holding of 87 acres. Until quite recently it was still being farmed by a resident family. Coins dating from the reign of James IV have been found in the sands.

The main road of North Uist skirts its north coast, passing between the white sands surrounding the tidal island of **Oronsay** and Loch nan Geireann. On one of the

Vallay Strand, North Uist

islands in the loch, Eilean-an-Tighe, the remains of a neolithic potter's workshop have been found. Acknowledged to be the earliest such example yet found in Western Europe, its size indicates it must have served quite a wide area. North Uist is rich in ancient sites; standing stones, stone circles and chambered cairns are spread profusely over the island. To the north of Grenitote, on the narrow peninsula of sand and machair, a team of archaeologists have excavated at Udal a site occupied from the Bronze Age until the Clearances. In the sea cliffs at the northern tip, Aird a' Mhòrain, an incised cross and some cup marks (Bronze Age carvings of ritual significance) have been found. A freshwater spring here is known as the Well of the Cross.

The tidal island of **Vallay** (which had a population of 59 in 1841) is reached across the white sands of Vallay Strand. The fine grey-stone house on the island was built by Erskine Beveridge and is now the property of the North Uist Estate.

At the north-west corner of North Uist is Griminish Point, where there is a natural rock arch 30 ft high. Eight miles west-north-west are **Haskeir Island** and **Haskeir Eagach**, a small group with stacks and arches, frequented by grey seals and puffins. Lewis Spence based his book, *Island of Disaster*, around Haskeir Eagach, the most southerly of the group. In Loch Scalpaig a small castellated folly stands on a green islet. It was built by Alex MacLeod, chamberlain to the MacDonald estates, who also erected the conspicuous Latin cross half a mile south-west at Kilphedder in 1830, after it was unearthed in a burial ground nearby. Beyond Loch Hosta (said to cover a drowned village) there is a vast area of dunes, and the small beach at Tràigh Stir, opposite the loch, is quite beautiful. In the cliffs at Tigharry is the Kettle Spout, a spouting cave.

To the west of Balranald House, once the seat of the MacDonalds of Griminish, is the RSPB's Balranald Reserve. The varied habitat here includes the tiny island of **Causamul**, two miles offshore, a seal nursery and refuge for the winter duck population, and beaches, dunes, machair, marshes and freshwater lochs. A notable rarity often seen here is the red-necked phalarope. Access to the reserve is restricted; the summer warden resides at Goular, near Hougharry.

Tigharry, Hougharry and Paible are the main west-coast communities, an area of well-kept crofts and grazing land. Many of the graves of North Uist's nobility are to be found in the churchyard at Hougharry. Inland, on the southern slope of South Clettraval (436 ft), is Cleatrbhal a' Deas, a wheelhouse and chambered cairn.

To the south of Paible there are wide expanses of white sand around the tidal dune islands of **Kirkibost Island** (across the sands from the solid, square Westford Inn) and the larger **Baleshare** reached by a causeway. Its name means East Township – West Township was swept away by the same exceptional tide that widened the Sound of Pabbay, and also isolated the Monach Isles (eight miles west of Baleshare) once fordable at low tide. There are extensive beaches on Baleshare, and the remains of Christ's Temple. Hugh MacDonald of Baleshare is thought to have introduced the kelp industry (kelp, when burned, produces alkali) to the Hebrides in about 1735, which resulted in a period of prosperity until it collapsed in the first half of the 19thC.

The most important ecclesiastical remains on North Uist are at Carinish in the extreme south-west. Here stands the fine ruin of Teampull na Trionaid, a medieval monastery and college thought to have been founded by Beathag, daughter of Somerled, in the early 13thC, and later enlarged by the wife of John MacDonald of Islay, first Lord of the Isles, in 1350. It was rebuilt in the 16thC, destroyed after the Reformation, and rebuilt again in the 19thC. Many chiefs sent their sons to be educated here. Alongside is Teampull Clan A'Phiocair, the chapel of the Macvicars, teachers at the college. Close by are the Slochdanan cup marks and Feithe na Fala, the Ditch of Blood, scene of a battle in 1601 between the MacLeods of Harris and the MacDonalds of Uist.

The main road south connects with Benbecula, but not before passing right through a stone circle on a slight rise, half a mile from Carinish. To the south of Loch Eport, the road through the small community of Locheport passes the five chambered cairns and stone circle of Croineubhal Craonaval, before finishing about one-and-a-half miles from the steep and rocky western side of Eaval which can only be climbed via its eastern slope (Loch Obisary cuts off any approach from the north and west.) The view from its summit is more than adequate compensation for the steep climb.

The road to the north of Loch Eport passes Ben Langass (295 ft), the only hill between Clachan and Lochmaddy. Conspicuous on its slope is Langass Barp, a neolithic chambered cairn which, although partially collapsed, can, with care, be entered. Around the western side of the hill can be found Pobull Fhinn, Finn's People, a stone circle above Loch Langass.

The western tip of the low-lying island of **Grimsay** is linked to North Uist (and Benbecula) by the causeway opened in 1960. Prior to its opening, the sands of Oitir Mhór (north ford) could be crossed at low tide, although not without risk as the tide rises swiftly. Grimsay is a lobster-fishing centre, with a large storage facility built in 1968. Live lobsters can be taken to the airport four miles away to arrive fresh in the fish markets within a few hours. Tweed is also woven here at Balaglas.

To the east of Grimsay the largest of several islands is **Ronay**, rising to a height of 377 ft, and uninhabited since the 1920s, although it once supported 180 people before being cleared in 1831. Fishermen were buried by the Lowlander's (St Michael's) Chapel.

Hostel accommodation is available at Lochmaddy (SYHA), Berneray and Claddach Baleshare (Gatliff Trust).

Benbecula

Benbecula's name derives from *Beinn a' bhfaodhla* (mountain of the fords), a reminder of days when the island was the stepping stone between the Uists. It is low-lying and windswept, with machair in the west and peat moorland in the east where the coast is deeply cut by sea lochs. The whole island is liberally endowed with freshwater lochs, making it, like its neighbours, a rewarding place for anglers and ornithologists.

There is a solitary hill, Rueval, a prominent landmark rising to 409 ft just north of the island's centre. On the south-east side of the hill is the cave where Bonnie Prince Charlie hid on 25 and 26 June 1746 while waiting for Flora MacDonald to organise his escape (see South Uist and Skye). The intrepid pair finally went over the sea to Skye from Rossinish, east of here. The easy walk to the top of Reuval is an excellent way to see the island, laid out like a map.

The indigenous population, a harmonious mixture of Protestant and Catholic numbering 1300 (plus 500 military personnel), have recently enjoyed a measure of prosperity thanks to the presence of the army at Balivanich. Whether these benefits will be long-term, and anything other than material, remains to be seen. The army base was established in 1958; in 1971 the missile range on South Uist and attendant facilities were expanded at a cost of £22 million. Initially, and understandably, there was local resistance to the military presence, but now the base has become an accepted part of the island's life to a degree that would leave a considerable vacuum were the Ministry of Defence to decide it were no longer needed.

Balivanich is the centre of activity on Benbecula – a cluster of regimented houses around the NAAFI building, with shops,

Benbecula, the 'mountain of the fords'

garages and other services, as well as a council office. To the north is the airfield, established by the RAF during World War II and now serving as an important link in the communications of these islands, with regular flights to Stornoway and Glasgow. It is manned by a small contingent of RAF technicians.

A main road crosses the island from north to south, but more interesting is the west-coast route which passes through the tidy crofts and farms. South of Balivanich is the Culla beach, beautiful cream sands backed by dunes, and behind these are the ruined walls of the 14thC Nunton Chapel. It was from Lady Clanranald at Nunton House that Bonnie Prince Charlie obtained his disguise as Betty Burke before leaving with Flora MacDonald from Rossinish on 28 June 1746. The road continues by the shore to Borve, where the ruined walls of the 14thC castle, once a Clan Ranald stronghold and occupied until 1625, stand in a field. To the south-west of the road are the barely visible remains of a chapel that once belonged to the castle. The MacDonalds of Clanranald held the island until 1839, when it was sold to Colonel Gordon of Cluny (see South Uist), whose family and trustees owned the island until 1942.

From Liniclate a minor road heads south-east to the pier at Peter's Port, with another road branching north to Loch Uiskevagh. The south-east coast here is in complete contrast to the west with many small coves and rocky islands, the largest being **Wiay**, a bird sanctuary, which in 1861 had a population of six, but has been uninhabited since 1901. The pier at Peter's Port was built in 1896; it was then found that there was no road to it, and access by sea was dangerous. Later a causeway and a road were built, but the pier was hardly ever used – and remains a planner's folly. The main road passes through Creagorry, with its hotel and large food store, before crossing O'Regan's Bridge (built in 1943 to serve the airfield) over the sands of South Ford to South Uist.

South Uist

The second largest island in the Outer Hebrides, having an area (including Benbecula and Eriskay) of 90,000 acres and a population of 2200, South Uist has a mountainous spine running almost the full length of its eastern side, rising to 2034 ft at the summit of Beinn Mhór and to 1988 ft at the summit of Hecla. Four sea lochs cut deep into the east coast: Loch Boisdale, Loch Eynort, Loch Skipport (joining with the non-tidal Loch Bee to make the north-east tip virtually an island) and Loch Sheilavaig. The west coast has 20 miles of virtually unbroken beach, white shell sand backed by dunes and the springy grass of the machair making for excellent coastal walking, usually with an invigorating salty breeze blowing off the clear, blue Atlantic. Between the mountains and the machair there is peaty moorland with many freshwater lochs, rich with salmon, sea trout and brown trout; however, fishing is strictly controlled. Here and there are deserted black houses, often looking more organic than man-made.

The main sources of income are crofting, fishing, fish and shellfish farming, alginates and the missile range. Seaweed is processed at North Lochboisdale, the wrack or tangle being collected from the east-coast bays, where great heaps are cast up after storms. Collection is done on a part-time basis, although the factory provides some full-time employment. The weed is also collected by crofters for their own use as fertiliser.

The Royal Artillery range is situated in the area west of West Gerinish and Loch Bee. It provides both direct employment, and work generated by the needs of the 500 or so military personnel. The islanders and soldiers are on good terms; compensation has been paid for land taken, and, when the range is not in use, the grazing is made available.

The Hebrideans of South Uist are mainly Roman Catholic – small roadside shrines are the visible evidence of this – and thus Sundays are a more lively affair than those on the Protestant islands further north.

The only village on the east coast is Lochboisdale (population 300) where the Caledonian MacBrayne vehicle ferry *Lord of the Isles* from Oban and Barra calls. There are shops, a hotel, bank, school, police station and Tourist Information Centre. The village straggles westward to Daliburgh, with crofts seemingly everywhere and cottages built quite often on rocky outcrops with scant regard for shelter – where the land is poor, the dwelling had to be built on the least fertile part of the croft.

Colonel Gordon of Cluny, who bought the island together with Benbecula and Eriskay from the MacDonalds of Clanranald (descendants of Ranald, the son of John, first Lord of the Isles) in 1838, was a particularly insensitive man. He cleared the islands for sheep, evicting crofters and forcing emigration. A few were given land on Eriskay which was too poor for sheep. During this period over 1000 emigrants left Lochboisdale on *The Admiral*, only to arrive in America destitute. Some of those evicted took to the hills, pursued by police. Between 1841 and 1861 the population of South Uist fell from 7300 to 5300. Later militant action by the crofters won them their present holdings. Today the whole 90,000 acre South Uist Estate is still privately owned.

At the mouth of Loch Boisdale is the island of **Calvay**, with a ruined 13thC castle where Bonnie Prince Charlie took refuge from the king's soldiers on 15 June 1746, and an automatic light replacing the original built in 1857. There is one main north-south road on South Uist which runs wide and straight beside the machair. It reveals little of the true character of the island, the most interesting parts of which are to be found by walking or driving down the narrow roads to the west and, occasionally, to the east.

South of Daliburgh, where there is a hospital, the main road finishes at Pollachar, the 'bay of the standing stone'. There is an inn here, with fine views towards Barra. South-west of Daliburgh, near Kilpheder, are the remains of a wheelhouse dating from the 2ndC AD, excavated in 1952. It has a circular plan, the hearth being the hub and stone piers at the rim supporting the spokes – wooden rafters. It was probably used as a farm house. Where the track from Kilpheder breaks into three near the sea, take the middle track. Over the dunes is a beautiful white beach. Further south along the main road, on a slight rise, is the church of Our Lady of Sorrows, built by the Barra priest Calum McNeil in 1963. The Garrynamonie school nearby will be long remembered for Frederick Rea, headmaster from 1890-1913, who refused to acknowledge Gaelic and taught only in English.

At Mingary, to the east of the road, a track leads to Barpa Mhingearraidh, a chambered cairn with a ring of pillar stones standing prominently on the slope of Reineval. Just north of Milton, a cairn inside low, ruined walls marks the birthplace of Flora MacDonald, the young woman who helped Bonnie Prince Charlie after his defeat at Culloden. The Prince left the mainland on 24 April 1746 with a price of £30,000 on his head. After many exploits in the Outer Hebrides, including being chased by a man o' war, and a three-day drunken debauch, he met Flora MacDonald, who agreed to help him. The Prince, disguised as Flora's maid 'Betty Burke', left Benbecula in a small boat for Skye on 28 June 1746. The ruin is worth visiting only for its romantic associations – there is nothing of interest to see.

About two miles north of Milton, a minor road ends at Rubha Ardvule, the most westerly point on the island. This promontory contains a small lochan, the haunt of many waterfowl. Beneath the shingle there is said to be an old Norse stone causeway, revealed once when exposed by a storm. By Loch Bornish there is a small Roman Catholic church with a simple and dignified interior, the only decoration being behind the altar. The minor road north through the crofts can be followed to Ormiclate Castle, a fine ruin standing in a farmyard. The unfortified building took seven years to build and burned down seven years later, on the eve of the Battle of Sherrifmuir in 1715, where the builder, Ailean MacDonald of Clanranald, was mortally wounded. Much still remains to be seen, including an armorial plaque in the north wall. Its site, overlooking the Atlantic, is superb.

The little church near the west coast at Howmore has an unusual central communion pew and a fine interior. Nearby are the remains of Caibeal Dhiarmaid church (dedicated to St Columba), Caibeal nan Sagairt and Teampull Mor. On an islet in Loch an Eilein are the few remains of Caisteal Bheagram, a small 15th - or 16thC tower. There is also a simple Gatliff Trust hostel at Howmore, near the church.

The ridge between the peaks of Beinn Mhór and Hecla dominates the area; a walk along the top is a fine energetic day's work with, of course, excellent views, including Skye and the Cuillins to the east. On the southern slope of Beinn Mhór, beneath the lower summit of Spin (1168 ft), is the wooded glen of Allt Volagir, full of birch and hazel, and brightened with violets and bluebells in the spring and Scottish primrose and Alpine gentian in summer.

The Loch Druidibeg National Nature Reserve (total area 4145 acres) is just to the north of Drimsdale, stretching four miles inland from the sandy shore, through the dunes and limey machair to the acid peat moorland around the loch. The shore of the loch is broken with many small peninsulas which, together with innumerable small islets, make an ideal habitat for many types of waterfowl. It is now the most important (and one of the last remaining) breeding grounds in the British Isles of the native grey lag goose. Also of interest is the differing flora of the two soil types; for instance the shallow calcaerous lochs and marsh of the machair have a richer vegetation than their counterparts in the acid peat. A rarity, the American pondweed, has its only natural distribution in the British Isles in the Uists. A permit is required to visit the reserve; the Nature Conservancy Council hostel is at Grogarry Lodge.

The road east to Loch Skipport, along the northern edge of the reserve, is well worth exploring. The country is rugged heather, peat and boulders, with a small clump of conifers and rhododendrons hiding around a corner as a pleasant surprise. There are lapwings everywhere. The road finishes with a steep descent to the decayed pier (built 1879) in the sheltered waters of Loch Skipport, where the steamers once called. The lighthouse at Rudha Ushinish became operational in 1857 and is now automatic. To the south is Nicolson's Leap, where legend has it that he leapt a 50 ft gap to the stack holding the Clanranald Chief's son in his arms, after a liaison with the chief's wife. From this perch he bargained with his pursuer, and ultimately jumped, with the boy, into the sea below.

Beyond the nature reserve, the army missile range begins to make its presence felt. A launching, if you happened to be there at the time (there are frequent periods of apparent inactivity), would be clearly visible from the perimeter. The missiles are

tracked from St Kilda, over 40 miles to the north-west.

On the slope of Rueval, The Hill of Miracles, is the 30-ft granite statute of Our Lady of the Isles by Hew Lorimer, erected in 1957 to commemorate Marian Year. The tall pillar-like Madonna and child look towards the missile range, and is itself overlooked by the range control installation (known as space city) at the summit.

The road crosses Loch Bee on a causeway. Mute swans can sometimes be seen on this large expanse of shallow water. It is noticeable that many of the small islets in the lochs throughout the Uists are covered with dense thickets of willow, hazel, rowan, and juniper growing among ferns, all thriving out of the reach of grazing sheep – an indication of what much of the island must have looked like before the hand of man fell so heavily upon it, clearing the trees and introducing sheep.

Eriskay

Eriskay (from the Gaelic *Eirisgeigh*, Eric's isle) is a small island, two-and-a-half by one-and-a-half miles, with a population of 200. The island was made famous worldwide by The Eriskay Love Lilt and other beautiful Gaelic melodies which originated here, and by the shipwreck of the SS *Politician*, which inspired Sir Compton Mackenzie's book, *Whisky Galore!* It also has its place in the romantic story of the ill-fated rising of 1745: the half-mile beach of Coilleag a' Phrionnsa on the west is where Bonnie Prince Charlie first set foot on Scottish soil, landing from *Du Teillay* en route from France to the Scottish mainland. The pink sea bindweed (*Calystegia soldanella*) which grows at the back of the beach, and on Vatersay, is said to have spread from seeds dropped by the Prince.

Eriskay

Eriskay belonged to the MacNeils of Barra until 1758, when it passed to the Mac-Donalds of Clanranald. Eriskay, Barra, Benbecula and South Uist were sold to Colonel Gorden of Cluny in 1838, who cleared the island for sheep but allowed a few evicted crofters to settle on Eriskay as it was too poor for grazing. Like the crofters of Harris, they made lazybeds of seaweed and peat, raised for drainage, on which they grew oats, barley and potatoes.

The main area of settlement is on the north coast, with another small township by the fine natural harbour in the east. The people of this thriving community are Roman Catholic, take great pride in their well-maintained and brightly painted houses, and have a strong attachment to their native island. There is a shop, primary school, post office and church. The main occupations, supplemented with crofting, are fishing (a small fleet takes herring, lobster, prawn and white fish) and the production by the women of hand-knitted sweaters, with patterns peculiar to Eriskay.

The sea around the island is quite shallow and unsuited to large vessels. It was therefore surprising when the 12,000-ton SS *Politician*, bound for New York with 24,000 cases of whisky on board, foundered to the east of Calvay, between Eriskay and South Uist. The islanders felt it their duty to salvage such a valuable cargo, and soon nearly everyone on the island, and some say the livestock as well, was drunk. What is less well known is that several islanders served prison sentences for possession of what was not theirs. Compton Mackenzie based his book *Whisky Galore!*, set on the fictional island of Todday, on these events. The classic Ealing comedy film of the same name was made on Barra in 1948. The seaweed-covered hulk of the stern of the ship is still visible at low tide, and a small pub on the island now commemorates the ship.

The angelus at St Michael's Church, built in 1903 by Father Allen MacDonald, is rung on a bell recovered from the German battle-cruiser *Derfflinger*, scuttled at Scapa Flow, and the altar base is constructed from the bow of a lifeboat from the aircraft-carrier

Hermes. Eriskay ponies, used on the island to carry peat and seaweed, are supposedly the nearest thing to a native Scottish breed still surviving. They stand 12 to 13 hands high, and have small ears but whether or not they are a native strain is not clear.

The ruin of Weaver's Castle on **Eilean Leathan** in the **Stack Islands**, off the southern tip, was once the base of the pirate and plunderer of wrecks, MacNeil. A vehicle ferry connects Eriskay with Ludag on South Uist.

Barra

Barra has a population of 1400, and an area of 22,000 acres (including Vatersay). It has been suggested that the name may derive from *Finbar* (St Barr), a 6thC saint. The island is a microcosm of the whole of the Outer Hebrides, with a rocky and broken east coast, fine sandy bays on the west backed with machair, rising to a maximum height of 1260 ft at the tooth-like summit of Heaval. The whole is Archaean gneiss, heavily glaciated. Over 150 species of birds and 400 types of plants have been recorded here – figures comparable with the rest of the Outer Hebrides.

Following the Norse domination of the Hebrides, the MacNeils held Barra from 1427, receiving the charter from Alexander, Lord of the Isles. James IV confirmed this charter in 1495. During the 16thC they

Outer Heisker

Sound of Mingula

Lianamul
Macphee's Hil
Mingulay B
Arnamul
Gunamul
Carnan
891'
MINGUL

Sound of Berneray

Skate
Point
BERNER

Barra Head

Soun
VA
He
F
Lin

raided English shipping, and made forays into Ireland. Athough taking no active part in the 1745 rising, the chief of the Clan Mac-Neil was implicated in the revolt, imprisoned, but never prosecuted; in 1747 the clan moved to Eoligarry. When in debt in 1838, Roderick MacNeil sold the island to Colonel Gordon of Cluny (who had also bought Ben-

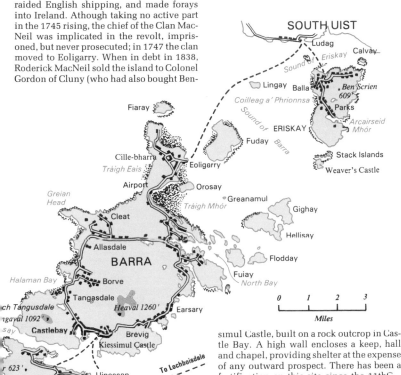

SOUTH UIST
Ludag
Calvay
Eriskay
Sound of
Lingay
Balla
Coilleag a' Phrionnsa
Ben Scrien
609'
Parks
Sound of
ERISKAY
Arcairseid
Mhór
Fuday
Barra
Stack Islands
Weaver's Castle
Fiaray
Cille-bharra
Tràigh Eais
Eoligarry
Airport
Orosay
Greian
Head
Cleat
Greanamul
Tràigh Mhòr
Gighay
Hellisay
Allasdale
Flodday
BARRA
Fuiay
Halaman Bay
Borve
North Bay
Tangasdale
ch Tangusdale
Heaval 1260'
Earsary
gaval 1092'
Castlebay
say
Brevig
Kiessimul Castle
r 623'
To Lochboisdale
Uidh
Uincasan
Vatersay Bay
To Oban
Vatersay
Muldoanich
Sound of Sandray
Cairn Galtar
678'
SANDRAY
Greanamul
und of Pabbay
ABBAY

0   1   2   3
Miles

becula, South Uist and Eriskay), who offered the island to the Government as a penal colony – a further demonstration of his total lack of sensitivity towards the islanders. Deciding he was receiving insufficient rent, he undertook clearances in 1857 with the help of imported policemen, confiscating the crofters' stocks and causing many emigrants to arrive destitute in the New World. Later land shortages led to discontent among the remaining crofters, with the result that the large farms were split.

The ancestral home of the MacNeils is the impressive medieval fortress of Kies-

simul Castle, built on a rock outcrop in Castle Bay. A high wall encloses a keep, hall and chapel, providing shelter at the expense of any outward prospect. There has been a fortification on this site since the 11thC – the present building dates from the 15thC. In 1937 Robert Lister MacNeil, 45th Chief of the Clan MacNeil, purchased his ancestral home together with 12,000 acres of Barra. An architect, he restored the castle, which has now become a focal point for MacNeils all over the world. He died in 1970 and is buried in the chapel. Enquire at the Tourist Information Centre if you wish to visit the castle.

The basis of the island's economy is crofting, with both sheep and cattle being kept. There is a growing fishing fleet catching white fish, prawns and lobster.

When James Methuen began using Castle Bay as a port in 1869, at the start of the herring boom, the associated curing and packing industries brought great prosperity. Within 20 years, as many as 450 boats, mainly from the east coast of mainland Scotland, were using the harbour, seeming to make a floating bridge to Vatersay. The resident fleet was ill-equipped to compete, but many Barra men were engaged as crew, and by 1911 the population of the island had risen to 2620. During the 1930s the industry declined, being halted finally by the outbreak of war.

The famous Sea League was formed here by Compton Mackenzie, who was then living on Barra, and John Lorne Campbell of Canna, in 1933, to protect local fishermen from illegal trawling in the Minch by the English. It pressed the Government for protective legislation but came up against stiff opposition from the English fishing lobby. Many young Barra men still go to sea, but now in either the merchant or Royal Navy or to the North Sea.

Other minor employment is found in the production of perfume, and knitwear, and the removal of shell grit from Tràigh Mhór, for use as a building material and as chicken feed. This latter activity is the subject of some debate, as it is claimed that the continuing removal of shell is compromising the future use of the beach as the island's airstrip.

Most of the people are Catholic, and have been so since St Patrick founded the See of the Isles in the 5thC, which, until the 14thC, was united with the See of Sodor and (Isle of) Man. During the 17thC there was a degree of religious persecution, but the islanders clung steadfastly to their faith. Ministers of the Church of Scotland have been present since 1734, and have been, for the most part, servile to the landowners, Rev. Henry Beatson (1847-71) particularly so during Colonel Gordon's clearances. Gaelic is spoken, although all the inhabitants are bilingual. The people are hardworking and unashamed in their pursuit of pleasure in contrast to their counterparts on Lewis. It is a very cheerful place, seven days a week.

The main settlement is Castlebay, served by Caledonian MacBrayne's *Lord of the Isles* from Oban and Lochboisdale Monday to Saturday, and *Iona* from Mallaig on summer Sundays. There are hotels, shops, a post office, Tourist Information Centre, schools, bank and hospital. A post bus runs to Eoligarry, via the east coast road. Castlebay faces south towards Vatersay, whilst sheltering it from the north

is the mountain of Heaval, with a statue of the Virgin and Child, erected in 1954, on its south-east slope. It is not a difficult walk to the top, and the view of the islands to the south is very fine. The large church overlooking Kiessimul Castle, Our Lady, Star of the Sea, was built in 1889. Moored by the castle is the lifeboat, which serves some of the most difficult waters around the coast of Britain.

The other main areas of settlement are North Bay, Eoligarry, Borve and Earsary. Eoligarry, north of Tràigh Mhór (known also as the Cockle Strand), is joined to the main body of the island by a neck of dunes. A small passenger ferry operates from the pier here to Ludag on South Uist. Above the grassland is Cille-bharra, the MacNeil burial ground. There are two roofless chapels by the restored church of St Barr, all possibly 12thC; Sir Compton Mackenzie is buried here. The views over the Sound of Barra to the mountains of South Uist are quite beautiful.

To the north of the long white beach of Tràigh Mhór, a few stones mark the site of Dun Scurrival, a prehistoric galleried fort. Off the northern-most tip is the low-lying island of **Fiaray**; to the east is the grassy island of **Fuday**, its name possibly deriving from the Norse *utey* (outside isle). This latter had a population of seven in 1861, although it has been deserted since the turn of the century. It was used for Norse burials, and was the retreat of some of King Haakon's forces after their defeat at the Battle of Largs in 1263.

The coast around North Bay is rocky and deeply indented. On an islet not far from the road stands a statue of St Barr by Margaret Somerville, a local artist, erected in 1975. The largest offshore island, **Hellisay**, had a population of 108 in 1841, but it was last occupied in the 1880s. The name is Norse – caves isle. Beyond Hellisay is **Gighay** (Gydha's isle), rising to a height of 305 ft; it also once had a small population. The road along the east coast winds around the many small bays, with lazybeds cram-

The Craigard Hotel and Our Lady, Star of the Sea, Barra

Eoligarry, Barra

med in everywhere – very reminiscent of south-east Harris.

The west coast between Greian Head and Doirlinn Head is a series of white sand beaches, with Halaman Bay in the south being outstanding – a magical place at sunset. Behind the sands is the machair, rich with flowers and scent in the spring and early summer. At Allasdale, to the north, are the remains of Dùn Cuier. Between Halaman Bay and Castle Bay, a path leads down to Loch Tangusdale (also called Loch St Clair), stocked with trout; the stump of Castle Sinclair, a small square tower, stands on an islet in the loch.

Barra's increasing population has made it possible for all essential services to be maintained. Even though limited employment prospects for young people lead to a degree of emigration, many people are returning and the future should harbour no fears for this particularly bright jewel of he Hebrides.

Vatersay

This is almost two islands, joined by a narrow neck of dunes and machair, with fine beaches in the bays thus formed. With a total population of 80, the main settlement is in the south – a picturesque shambles of cottages, wooden council houses, abandoned vehicles and grazing cattle. There is a post office and a public call-box here. To the north is the junior school, community centre, chapel and a few scattered cottages all linked by narrow metalled roads.

The economy is based on cattle and sheep. Until quite recently the cattle were tethered to boats and swum across to Barra, to be taken by the Caledonian MacBrayne ferry to the market at Oban. They are now transported by barge, with the result that they arrive at the market in a better condition.

The population in 1861 was 32, but by 1911 it had risen to 288 due to an influx of immigrants from Barra and Mingulay. After falling to around 70 people and seeming to lose impetus in the early 1970s, it climbed to 100 but has again diminished to 60 or so. Totally dependent upon Barra for medical services, secondary schooling and entertainment, many of the younger people have moved across the Sound of Vatersay to the larger island. A *planned* £3 million causeway to Barra seems to provide the only means of ending depopulation.

At the turn of the century Vatersay was run as a single farm by tenants of Lady Gordon Cathcart, who only visited the island once during her 54 years of ownership. This was at a time of severe land shortage on Barra and South Uist. After pressure from the crofters, the Lady grudgingly parted with a small area of land at Eoligarry on

Barra. Continuing unrest forced the Congested Districts Board to try to buy land on Vatersay to rent to the crofters. Finally, in desperation, on the 19 August 1906, one crofter, within one day, erected a wooden dwelling on Vatersay Farm, thatched it and lit a fire; under ancient law this gave him title to the land. Others followed suit. These Vatersay Raiders were brought to trial, but were subsequently released after a public outcry. In 1909 the Board finally purchased the whole island and divided it into 58 holdings.

The island rises to 625 ft at the summit of Heishival Mór. Off the extreme eastern tip is the small tidal island of **Uinessan**, where once stood the church of Cille Bhrianain, known as Caibeal Moire nan Ceann, the chapel of Mary of the heads – a short-tempered lady who decapitated those who upset her. Two miles to the east, the dark hump of **Muldoanich** rises from the sea. It once had a chapel and was known in Gaelic as Maol Domhnaich, the island of the tonsured one of the Lord.

To the west of Vatersay, in 1853, 450 emigrants, many of them Hebrideans, lost their lives when the *Annie Jane* was wrecked. To the south of Vatersay all the islands, once known as the Bishop's Isles, are uninhabited. Enquire at Castlebay for details of trips. The Western Isles Council run a sturdy passenger ferry from Castlebay pier to Vatersay. This stretch of water can, at times, be very rough.

Sandray

The name means sand isle. It lies about one-half mile south of Vatersay, rising to a height of 678 ft at the summit of Cairn Galtar. A strip of dunes lies parallel to the east coast. In the early 18thC, the island was divided into nine farms; by 1881 the population had fallen to ten, but rose to 41 in 1911 due to resettlement. It had been deserted since 1934. There was once an ancient chapel, known as Cille Bhride, on the island. To the west, are the small islands of **Lingay, Greanamul** and **Flodday**, the last having a natural arch.

Pabbay

Two-and-a-half miles south-west of Sandray, this is one of the many Priest's Isles in the Hebrides, with the summit rising to a height of 561 ft, steep sea cliffs and a massive arched overhang. In 1881 the population was 26 with the settlement being on the eastern side above a shell sand beach. On 1 May 1897 all the able-bodied men were lost in a fierce storm at sea whilst long lining. The Mingulay boat survived the same storm. The island is now deserted. On the north-east corner are the remains of Dùnan Ruadh,

the red fort, and above Bàgh Bàn there was once a chapel and burial ground – still remaining are three cross-marked stones and one with a cross, a crescent and a lily. All are possibly Pictish. Some small islands lie to the south-west.

Mingulay

Taking its name from the Norse for big isle, Mingulay lies two miles south-west of Pabbay, and is two-and-a-half miles by one-a-and-half miles. It was once owned by Mac-Neil of Barra, who took care of his tenants – finding new wives for widowers, new husbands for widows, and making good the loss of any milking cow. The remains of the settlement can be seen on the east side, above the sandy Mingulay or Village Bay; the population peaked at 150 in 1881 when the island had its own school, but fell rapidly in the 1900s when many of the inhabitants joined the Vatersay Raiders. By 1934 the population numbered two, and it is now deserted.

On the western side, the sea cliffs are magnificent, Biulacraig being a sheer 700 ft. Islanders once climbed these crags to harvest seabirds' eggs. There are many seabirds, including a large puffin colony, nesting among the ledges, stacks and caves. Two islets off the west coast, **Arnamul** and **Lianamul**, were once grazed by sheep, the latter being reached by a rope bridge.

The highest point is Carnan, rising to 891 ft. Macphee's Hill (735 ft) is named after a rent collector who landed on the island and found all the inhabitants dead from the plague. His companions rowed away in fear, leaving the unfortunate man on his own for a year, but MacNeil of Barra gifted him some land when the island was resettled. A Bronze Age stone cist (burial chamber), Crois an t'Suidheachain, has been uncovered on the island.

Berneray

The southernmost island of the Outer Hebrides and known as Barra Head, its tall sea cliffs (over 600 ft at Skate Point) take the full brunt of the Atlantic waves, unbroken by shallow water. After severe gales, small fish are sometimes found on the grass at the top, and in 1836 a 42-ton rock was moved five feet by the force of a storm.

At the western end stands the Barra Head lighthouse, 680 ft above sea level, marking the end, or the beginning, of the Outer Hebrides. Granite to build the tower was quarried on the island. Near the lighthouse are the remains of two promontory forts. In 1881 the population was 57; now that the lighthouse is automatic, the island is unpopulated. The name Berneray is from the Norse, Bjorn's isle.

The Hebridean outliers

Flannan Isles

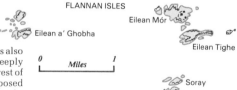

FLANNAN ISLES

Eilean a' Ghobha

Eilean Mór

Eilean Tighe

Soray

0 Miles 1

These are a group of cliff-bound islands also known as The Seven Hunters, rising steeply from the sea to 288 ft, 21 miles north-west of Gallan Head, Lewis. They are composed of hornblende gneiss, and have an area of a little under 100 acres.

On the largest island, **Eilean Mór** (38 acres), are the remains of the 8thC Chapel of St Flannan, and a lighthouse built 1899 by D. & C. Stevenson of Edinburgh – the scene of a mystery rivalling that of the *Marie Celeste*. On the night of 15 December 1900, a passing steamer, the *Archer*, reported to the Northern Lighthouse Board that the light was out. The *Hesperus* was sent to investigate. The landing party could find no trace of the three keepers: James Ducat, Thomas Marshall and Donald MacArthur. Ducat's logbook was complete up to 13 December, and a slate continued the record to 9.00 a.m. on the 15th. Ducat's and Marshall's oilskins were gone, a meal of cold meat, pickles and potatoes for three lay untouched, and one chair was knocked over.

The weather at the time of the disappearance was foul, to the extent that a crane was torn from its foundations 100 ft above sea level, and a concrete structure was demolished. The logbook told of damage to the west landing, an inlet finishing in a cave, called Skiopageo. The most common theory is that Ducat and Marshall went to inspect this landing. MacArthur, seeing a freak wave coming, ran to warn them. The wave burst into the inlet, exploded in the cave and swept all three away.

The story became well known in the early 1900s with the publication of Wilfred Gibson's poem Flannan Isle: 'Three men alive on Flannan Isle/Who thought on three men dead.' The light is now automatic. An old rail track, used for transporting fuel, climbs steeply up the cliffs to the tower.

During the 16thC the MacLeods of Lewis used to visit the Flannans to hunt wild sheep and collect seabirds' eggs after performing an elaborate rite of prayer, and not calling anything by its proper name. Today a few sheep are still grazed on the grassy tops by Lewis crofters.

Shiant Isles

The name comes from *Na h-eileanan seunta* (the enchanted isles). This is a small group ten miles east-north-east of Scalpay, Harris. **Garbh Eilean** (rough island) and **Eilean an**

Tighe (home island) are joined by a narrow neck of land; the third island is **Eilean Mhuire** (Mary's island). On the north and east sides there are spectacular sea cliffs of columnar basaltic formation rising to over 400 ft. Compared with the ancient gneiss of the Outer Hebrides, this is young rock, a geological relative of the islands of Staffa and Mull.

Eilean Mhuire

Garbh Eilean

SHIANT ISLANDS

Eilean an Tighe

410'

0 Miles 1

They were last inhabited, by eight people, in 1901. In 1845 a whole family fell to their death while hunting sea birds on the cliffs of Garbh Eilean. The islands were owned at one time by Sir Compton MacKenzie, who renovated the house on Eilean an Tighe and spent some time there writing. In 1937 they were sold to the author and publisher, Nigel Nicolson, for £1500.

The islands support large colonies of puffins (which burrow into the cliffs), guillemots and wintering barnacle geese. The scree at the foot of the cliffs harbours many brown rats, and the islands are grazed by sheep.

A boat can be hired from Tarbert or Scalpay to visit the Shiants, but beware of the legendary Blue Men of the Minch, who live in the Sound of Shiant and are said to be not particularly friendly.

St Kilda

This is a spectacular group of islands and stacks, 41 miles west-north-west of Griminish Point, North Uist, owned by the National Trust for Scotland and designated a World Heritage Site. The largest island, **Hirta**, has an area of 1575 acres. The origins of the names *Kilda* and *Hirta* are not clear, since there is no known saint called Kilda. The Norse for 'well' is childa. Hirta mispronounced with the characteristic St Kildan lisp would have been spoken as 'Hilta', and possibly confused with 'childa' by fishermen calling to replenish their supplies at the well. The 'St' was thought to have been added due to the common religious associations of wells and springs.

Soay and **Dun** close by are 244 and 79 acres respectively, with **Boreray** (189 acres), **Stac an Armin** (13 acres) and **Stac Lee** (96 acres) forming a separate group four miles north-east. All of the islands are formed from volcanic rock – granite and gabbro – rising to a height of 1397 ft at the grassy summit of Conachair, Hirta; 1225 ft at the summit of Soay; and 1260 ft on Boreray. Exposure to the full erosive force of the Atlantic has resulted in sheer sea cliffs over 1000 ft high, the most magnificent in Britain. At the base of these walls of rock are many caves, stacks and arches - note especially that in Geo na h-Airde, the most spectacular natural arch on the islands. In the Boreray group, Stac an Armin (622 ft) is the tallest monolith in the British Isles.

St Kilda was inhabited for possibly 2000 years by a hardy and, for the majority of that time, self-sufficient community, until the evacuation in 1930. It is known that the Vikings visited these islands. Their original settlement was at Glen Bay (known to the army as Seal Bay) on the north side, where there are shielings (summer grazings with rudimentary shelters) to be seen. The most recent population centre was at Village Bay, with some remains of a previous settlement behind. Arable land was enclosed by a dyke. Among the dwellings, and scattered up the mountain slopes, are cleits – small dry-stone and turf-roofed structures used for storing dried sea birds which were the St Kildans' staple diet.

The earliest buildings at Village Bay were pulled down for the building of new black houses in 1830. The present cottages along the main street, which are being progressively restored, are of the but-and-ben type, built about 1860. To the east of the houses are the manse (occupied by the army), the school (built 1899) and the church (built in the 1830s), all lovingly restored by working parties recruited by National Trust for Scotland and which have been coming here for more than 20 summers. The remains of one rude hut are known as Lady Grange's House – an unfortunate woman exiled on the island for eight years from 1734 for threatening to reveal her husband's Jacobite sympathies prior to the '45 Rising. She died in 1745 and is buried at Trumpan, on Skye.

The population of St Kilda numbered 180 in 1697, but there was a steady decline from this peak, with several low points during cholera and smallpox outbreaks. From the 1750s to the early 1920s the community numbered over 70.

The islands were owned by the MacLeods of Harris and Dunvegan (in Skye) who were given them by a successor of Ranald, son of John, Lord of the Isles. Rent was paid by the St Kildans in the form of tweed, feathers, wool, dairy produce, stock, oil and

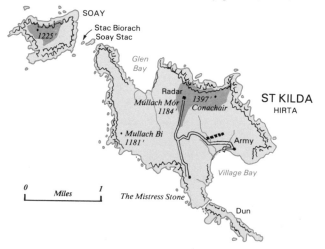

SOAY

Stac Biorach
Soay Stac

Glen Bay

1225

Radar
Mullach Mór   1397
1184'   Conachair

Mullach Bi
1181'

Army

Village Bay

The Mistress Stone

Dun

ST KILDA
HIRTA

0   Miles   1

grain. A steward was appointed by the Mac-Leods, and his deputy lived on the island, and once a year the steward himself visited to collect the rent.

The islanders held in common ownership everything that was vital to their existence, and all produce was shared. Each day the St Kilda Parliament would meet, latterly outside the post office, to discuss the day's tasks. With no one man having ascendency over the others, these discussions could go on all day, with nothing decided. There was no insobriety, but among the men there was a marked fondness for tobacco. Crime was unknown.

Along with the usual crofting activities such as peat cutting, tending the stock, fishing, harvesting, building, sewing, spinning and weaving, the St Kildan men collected thousands of sea birds and their eggs. Working in teams using horse-hair ropes, they scaled the terrifying cliffs and stacks (including those of Boreray, a hazardous boat

Stac an Armin

BORERAY

ac Lee

journey away) in their stockinged feet, with remarkably few accidents. Their ankles became thick and strong, and their toes prehensile. They took young gannets, puffins (for their feathers only) and most importantly, fulmars, the bodies of which provided oil for their lamps and for export – one-half pint of oil from each bird. Typical yearly harvests might be 5000 gannets, 20,000 puffins, 9000 fulmars. After plucking, the feathers were sorted, and the carcasses salted and packed for storage in the cleits. Nothing was wasted – even the entrails were used as manure.

There were two tests of climbing ability and agility used by the St Kildans. Young men had to scale Stac Biorach, 236 ft high, in Soay Sound, regarded as the stiffest climb in the group; and, before marriage, each suitor had to balance on one heel on the mistress stone at the south-west of St Kilda, perched high above the sea, while grasping his other foot with his hands. This proved his prowess as a collector of food.

Apart from the ravages of contagious disease, the population was a healthy one, although it is not surprising that dyspepsia was common as their diet consisted largely of the oily flesh of sea birds. Perhaps the most tragic disease to afflict the island was 'eight-day sickness', *tetanus infantus*,

which claimed eight out of every ten children born in the years before 1838. Various church ministers claimed it to be God's will, and the island people accepted this. Fortunately the Rev. Angus Fiddes did not. He took a course in midwifery and returned to St Kilda in the 1890s determined to eradicate the disease. He found that St Kildans traditionally coated the severed umbilicus of an infant with a mixture of fulmar oil and dung, and were loathe to change their ways. After a protracted battle with the islands' knee woman who performed this rite, he demonstrated that by using sterile and antiseptic methods this centuries-old blight could be eradicated.

The arrival of the first tourists aboard the steamship *Glen Albyn* in July 1834 marked the start of the St Kildan's increased dependence on the outside world, and their subsequent decline. They sold cloth, skins and birds' eggs and used the money thus earned to buy food, clothing and tobacco. This commerce, a new factor in their economy, depended on good communications with the mainland – communications that were difficult to maintain due to the weather conditions and their situation en route to nowhere.

During the latter part of the 19thC the St Kildans relied on the prevailing westerly winds to carry messages requesting help to the main Hebridean islands. They fashioned small wooden boats with masts and sails, or used inflated sheeps' bladders, with the letters enclosed in bottles. Later, a loose arrangement was made with trawlermen to convey messages and mail. The post office on the island was opened in 1899, but there were never any scheduled deliveries or collections.

Other factors influencing the eventual evacuation were education, which began in earnest in 1884 and taught the young people that there might be a better life elsewhere, and a series of resident ministers who inspired such religious zeal that the islanders were in church every day of the week, at times when they should have been growing or collecting food.

After the community nearly starved in 1912 a wireless transmitter was installed the following year, although it soon broke down. It was repaired and used during World War I, resulting in a German submarine shelling the island on 18 May 1918, destroying the store and damaging the church, but harming no one. The submarine was later captured by an armed trawler. A cannon, which can be seen to the east of the army camp, was later positioned to guard the bay. It was never fired.

Finally, a decision was taken and the island was evacuated on 29 August 1930, when 36 St Kildans left on HMS *Harebell* with those cattle and sheep that could be

The Village, St Kilda. *National Trust for Scotland*

rounded up following on the *Dunara Castle*, a ship which had been bringing tourists out to *the edge of the world* since 1875. Most of the St Kildan men, on leaving an island with no trees, were found work with the Forestry Commission.

The Nature Conservancy Council and the Army now manage the islands, Britain's premier sea-bird breeding station, in partnership with the National Trust for Scotland. It has been estimated that 37 per cent of the total world gannet population is to be found there, particularly on Stac an Armin and Stac Lee. There were 59,000 breeding pairs counted during the period 1971-74, as well as 40,000 pairs of fulmars, the largest single British colony, and 150,000 pairs of puffins – about half the British total. Figures on the storm petrel are not clear, but the colony is thought to be one of the largest. Also to be found breeding are Manx shearwater, Leach's petrel, razorbill and great skua, but there are only seven species of land birds breeding on the group, including the St Kilda wren, a sub-species. There is also a species of long-tailed field-mouse peculiar to the group, although the St Kilda house-mouse died out soon after the evacuation.

Between 600 to 2000 Soay sheep (the population is cyclical) roam free on St Kilda; they are a primitive species similar to those kept by neolithic farmers. Where the sheep cannot graze, the vegetation on Dun is particularly lush. On Boreray the sheep left by the St Kildans, blackface and cheviot crosses, have reverted to a wild state. Over 130 flowering plants occur, including some mountain types influenced by the cool climate. Wind speeds of 130 mph at sea level have been recorded.

Since 1957, the army have maintained a £1 million base of 40 men to run the missile-tracking radar on top of Mullach Mór. Supplies and mail are delivered by landing craft, helicopter and air drop, and the men are in constant radio contact with the firing range on South Uist. Even so, they are sometimes isolated for weeks on end in bad weather. The army regularly assists the National Trust for Scotland in their work, and their presence (and power supply) is greatly appreciated by the resident summer warden.

Those who have spent 24 hours or more on, or have sailed to, St Kilda can join the exclusive St Kilda Club. Artefacts and memorabilia of the St Kildans can be seen in a small museum in one of the cottages, and you can visit the army's 'Puff Inn'. But the St Kildans themselves are no more – a community which became an administrative inconvenience and a charge upon mainstream society has been lost for ever for want of many of the things that are now provided by the army. Those wishing to land on the island *must* first contact the National Trust for Scotland.

Stac an Armin and Boreray

Monach Islands

Also known as Heisker, these are a group of four small islands about eight miles west of Baleshare, South Uist, with a total area of 836 acres. The two main ones, **Ceann Iar** and **Ceann Ear** (where there was once a convent) are joined at low tide.

On **Shillay**, the most westerly, there is a red brick lighthouse, built in 1864 but disused since 1942; at one time a crude light was maintained by monks who inhabited the islands. In the 16thC, sands that were passable at low tide between the Monachs and North Uist were swept away by the same exceptional tide that formed the Sound of Pabbay.

The islands have long been populated. Before 1810 over 100 people lived there, but overgrazing weakened the stabilising grass, and a disastrous storm blew the top soil away and the people left. By 1841, 19 people were re-established, and in 1891 over 100 people were again living on the group with their own post office and school. The numbers then began to dwindle and the last crofters left in 1942; the only cottage still habitable is privately owned. Occasionally the islands are visited by lobster fishermen. A cairn on Ceann Iar marks the grave of Lieut. R.N.R. MacNeill, who drowned as a result of H.M.A. *Laurentic* striking a mine on 25 January 1917 off Northern Island. Superstitious sailors believe their drowned body will drift home – in the case of Lieut. MacNeill this was indeed the case, since Ceann Iar is the traditional clan home.

The Monachs are now a National Nature Reserve, and permission to land must be obtained from the North Uist Estate, Lochmaddy, and from the warden at Loch Druidibeg. The habitat is a prime example of shell sand, dune and uncultivated machair over gneiss; the rock rises only to a little over 60 ft. Barnacle and white-fronted geese winter here, and arctic, common and little terns, fulmars and herons may also be seen. The reef of **Stockay** is a grey-seal nursery.

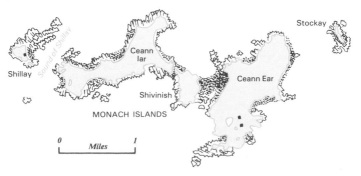

Shillay

Sound of Shillay

Ceann Iar

Shivinish

Stockay

Ceann Ear

MONACH ISLANDS

0   Miles   1

The north west

Handa Island

Highland. This mainly cliffbound island of 766 acres consists of a Torridonian sandstone outcrop standing off a Lewisian gneiss foreland, less than a mile south-west of Tarbet. The sea cliffs on the north and west rise to 400 ft, and there is an impressive rock known as the Great Stack, resting on three pillars. The interior is mainly rough pasture, peat bog and heather. It was once inhabited by seven families who had a 'queen' and, as on St Kilda, the menfolk used to hold a daily parliament to decide the work. The people emigrated to America during the potato famine of 1848. Handa was used as a burial place by mainlanders to save the corpses from scavenging wolves.

Although privately owned, Handa is run as a nature reserve by the RSPB who maintain a warden during the summer. 141 species of bird have been recorded, with 35 breeding regularly. Of most importance are the colonies of sea birds. The last white-tailed sea eagles nested here in 1864. Of great notoriety was an eccentric albino oystercatcher with a deformed bill, which died on 9 July 1967 and is now in the Royal Scottish Museum, Edinburgh. 216 species of plants have been recorded plus more than 100 species of mosses. Small plantations of lodgepole pine and alders have been established, and there are many rabbits.

A bothy is available to those who wish to stay on the island (book with RSPB in Edinburgh), and day visits can be made via a local boatman in Tarbet (not Suns). A modest landing fee is charged.

Summer Isles

Highland. These are a group of islands and skerries spread over 30 square miles, lying north-west of Loch Broom, consisting of Torridonian sandstone covered with peat.

The largest island in the group is **Tan-era Mór**, with an area of 804 acres. In 1881 its population numbered 119 people, who lived in the settlements by The Anchorage, one of the best natural harbours in the north-west. The population declined until, in 1931, the last tenants left. Sir Frank Fraser Darling farmed the island between 1939 and 1944, and wrote about this period in his book *Island Farm*. Then once again it was deserted until the mid-1960s, when the Summer Isles Estate decided to restore many of the cottages and the schoolhouse as holiday accommodation. The permanent population now numbers about 10, and 250 sheep are grazed. The Summer Isles Post Office, which issues its own stamps (recognised by the Post Office) for conveying mail to the mainland, and the Offshore Islands Philatelic Society are both run from Tanera Mór.

Between the settlements of Ardnagoine and Garadheancal are the remains of a fishing station at Tigh-on-Quay founded in 1783 by Roderick Morison of Stornoway and John Mackenzie of London, whose business thrived when the seas were full of herring; there were other stations on **Isle Ristol** and Isle Martin. Barrels of the salted fish were exported as far afield as the West Indies, and as many as 200 vessels were at one time to be seen anchored in the bay. During the 19thC the island was a centre for the illicit distilling of whisky. Tanera Mór rises to 405 ft at the summit of Meall Mór, affording fine views as far as the Outer Hebrides. Holiday accommodation can be booked through the Summer Isles Estate, and a regular ferry operates from Achiltibuie. There are facilities for boating, sailing and fishing among other things, amid excellent scenery and seclusion.

The island of **Tanera Beg**, to the west, has a beach of coral sand, rare in this area. **Horse Island**, once inhabited, now supports only a herd of wild goats, first recorded in 1937. To the south-south-west is **Carn nan Sgeir**, two islets joined by a shingle spit. Orange, grey and black lichens hide the cliffs, and the ledges are covered with thrift, sea campion, scurvygrass and lovage.

The most westerly of the group are **Priest Island** (or Eilean à Chleirich, 300 acres), and the much smaller **Glas-leac Beag** (34 acres). There is no proper landing place on Priest Island and its exposed position makes access difficult – in spite of this, it was at one time occupied by a crofting family, originally an outlaw banished from the mainland. The third generation of this fam-

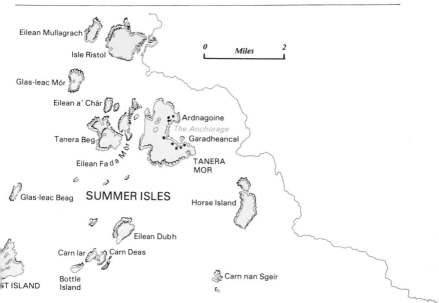

Eilean Mullagrach
Isle Ristol
Glas-leac Mór
Eilean a' Chàr
Ardnagoine
The Anchorage
Tanera Beg
Garadheancal
Eilean Fada
TANERA MOR
Glas-leac Beag
SUMMER ISLES
Horse Island
Eilean Dubh
Carn Iar
Carn Deas
Carn nan Sgeir
Bottle Island
T ISLAND
ISLE MARTIN

0   *Miles*   2

ily left in the mid-19thC. Sir Frank Fraser Darling, naturalist, wrote about his stay on this island in *Island Years*. On its summit are three stone circles and seven small lochs. It is now notable for its colonies of storm petrels and otters. It was recently bought for the RSPB, but there is no visiting.

All of these islands are now rich in bird life – heron, shelduck, fulmar, snipe, and eider are among the species commonly seen – and many are still grazed by sheep. There are boat trips from Archiltibuie and Ullapool, but most of the islands are privately owned.

Isle Martin lies to the east of the Summer Isles, to the north of Loch Broom, and is composed of Torridonian sandstone, with an area of 390 acres and a maximum elevation of 393 ft. In the late 18thC, at the start of the herring boom, the British Fisheries Society erected a curing station close by Ardmair Bay, the foundations of which still exist. In 1901 the population of the island was 33, but by the start of World War II the last resident had left. Mrs Monica Goldsmith bought the island in 1965, restoring the four houses and preserving it from development. She later gave it to the RSPB to manage as a reserve – of particular interest are the heronry, the tern colony, red-breasted mergansers, eiders, oystercatchers and ringed plovers. There is a legend about a cooper of Isle Martin who was miraculously transported to South Rona to cut brooms and then equally miraculously brought back – all, of course, arranged by the fairies. There are trips around the Summer Isles from both Achiltibuie and Ullapool. Ullapool is also

the terminus for the Caledonian MacBrayne vehicle ferry *Suilven* to Stornoway, Isle of Lewis.

Gruinard Island

Highland. This island lies in the attractive Gruinard Bay, its name deriving from the Norse *grunna fjord* (shallow ford). During World War II it was used as a test site for biological weapons. The last inhabitants had left long before these experiments were carried out. During 1986 a cleaning up operation was undertaken, spraying the contaminated areas with formaldehyde and sea water, effectively surrounding any anthrax spores left in the soil in a chemical coffin, making the island safe, and the warning notices unnecessary.

A generally low-lying sandstone island in Loch Ewe, half a mile from Aultbea, the **Isle of Ewe** rises to 223 ft at its northern tip, and 232 ft in the west.

In Loch Gairloch, **Eilean Horrisdale** shelters the jetties of Aird and Badochro, and to the north of the loch is the sandstone **Longa Island**, sheltering the beach of Big Sand. To the south are Lochs Torridon and Shieldaig, the latter containing tiny **Shieldaig Island** which was purchased by the National Trust for Scotland in 1970, and adopted in 1974 by Mr and Mrs Armistead Peter III of Washington, D.C., who contributed a sum equivalent to the full purchase price. In the 19thC this island had been planted with Scots pine, which, with a few rowans and some holly, now make a welcome contrast to the surrounding barren hills.

The mainland coast to Applecross is bare and mountainous – splendid walking country. To the south of this village, **Eilean nan Naomh** shelters Camusterrach harbour. Little more than a rocky outcrop, this is the Holy Isle where St Maolrubha is said to have landed in AD 671; he founded a monastery at Applecross, which was later destroyed by the Vikings. To the south there are a few islets and rocks. About a mile south-west of Loch Toscaig, the **Crowlin Islands** are reached, a volcanic outcrop with a north-south split giving a sheltered central channel 50-yds wide. The largest of the three islands is **Eilean Mór**, rising to a summit of 374 ft, which has some ruined cottages in the north-east corner. A lighthouse stands on the smallest island, **Eilean Beag**, and its shoreline, rocky and with caves, is inhabited by both common and Atlantic seals. Regular summer boat-trips are made from the Kyle of Lochalsh. The waters of the Inner

Sound, to the north, are the deepest off the immediate coast of Britain; Royal Navy torpedo tests are made here.

Eilean na Creige Duibhe is a Scottish Wildlife Trust conservation area where herons nest by fine Scots pines. Visits can be made by boat from Plockton.

Eilean Bàn (white island) lies off Kyle of Lochalsh, with a pretty white lighthouse (now automatic) at its western end. The white painted cottages were built for the keepers and their families who once tended the light. The late Gavin Maxwell, author of *Ring of Bright Water*, bought the island in 1963 intending to turn it into a private zoo for Scottish wildlife. He converted the two cottages into one, and moved to the island in 1968 after his house at Sandaig on the mainland burned down. Ill-health prevented him realising this plan and, after living for a while at Kyle House on Skye, he died in Broadford Hospital on 7 September 1969. His otter, Teko, the last survivor from the *Ring*, is buried beneath a boulder on Eilean Bàn. The island, which now has its own swimming pool and sauna, is privately owned, having recently changed hands for £75,000.

Island of Skye

Highland. The name Skye derives from the Norse *skuy*, meaning cloud; in Gaelic it is *Eilean à Cheo* (isle of mist). Easy access, breathtaking scenery and romantic associations with Bonnie Prince Charlie have made Skye popular since Victorian times, when the new railway to Stromeferry opened up the island. The Victorians came to walk, watch birds, collect fossils and flowers and to paint, and it says much for the timeless quality of the island that visitors today do much the same.

The island (with a population of 7000) is 48 miles long, 24 miles wide (as far as its shape allows determination), and has an area of 430,000 acres. Near the centre are the magnificent Cuillin Hills, the most dramatic manifestation of the volcanic activity which shaped the bulk of the island, formed from the solidified reservoir from which the lavas flowed some 40 million years ago (during the Tertiary period). These granite mountains culminate in extremely sharp ridges of pointed rock, like an edge made of broken china above the dark grey slopes. This rock is extremely hard and owes its present form to its (relatively) young age and the abrasive effect of ice. The Red Cuillins were formed 2700 million

years ago (during the Lewisian period) and as a consequence have been subjected to prolonged weathering – hence their more rounded appearance. Give the Cuillins another 2660 million years and they too will look like this!

The north of the island, including Duirinish, Waternish and half of Trotternish, was formed from a succession of lava flows, giving the land a stepped appearance, seen clearly on Macleod's Tables – Healabhal Bheag and Healabhal Mhor – where softer outpourings have been eroded leaving the characteristic flat tops and tiered slopes. The oldest rock on Skye, gneiss, is found in Sleat (pronounced slate), south of Isleornsay, with old red sandstone forming the rest of the peninsula.

In Trotternish, the Quiraing and the Old Man of Storr are the remains of volcanic rock which was left stranded on top of soft clays when the glaciers melted – the softer material giving way, leaving the blocks to slip down, creating cliffs and ravines.

Underlying sandstones, limestones and clays surface around the volcanic rock to give the best soils on the island, and this has generally determined human settlement. Northern Trotternish, Broadford and the

Opposite: The Skye Cuillin from Portnalong

west of Loch Slapin are typical of these areas, with many farms and crofts. Some places of lush green vegetation behind Broadford mark the limestone outcrops. Where this limestone was baked by volcanic activity, marble has been produced, and it is still quarried near Torrin.

There are coral beaches at Claigan on Loch Dunvegan, formed by the seaweed *Lithothamnion*, and to the south of Duntulm Castle in Trotternish the sand has a green tint due to the sea eroding the mineral, olivine, from the cliffs. Gold has also been found on the island.

There are 20 peaks in the Cuillins, 15 over 3000-ft high with the highest, Sgurr Alasdair, being 3257 ft. The first to be climbed, in 1836, was Sgurr nan Gillean (3167 ft), by a geologist named Forbes. Sgurr a' Ghread-aidh, at 3190 ft, is ascended from the Loch Coruisk side, one of the longest rock climbs in Britain.

Much of the island landscape is empty, with small crofting townships of scattered cottages only where the soil is workable. There are many ruined houses and empty glens, evidence of the Jacobites who were forced to leave after the unsuccessful rising of 1745, the bad harvests of 1881-85 and the Clearances.

A croft is a small farm usually of five to ten acres. The original crofters were self-sufficient, occupying arable land, divided into small areas, on a rotation basis, and sharing hill grazing.

This way of life ended for many with the introduction of large-scale sheep farming, often by absentee landlords and the clearance of the crofters from the land. Whole townships were evicted and forced to emigrate to the New World; between 1840 and 1888 over 30,000 people left. By 1882 over 365,000 acres of Skye were owned by absentee landlords, and it was then that things came to a head when crofters at The Braes were denied grazing rights they considered theirs. A force of 50 Glasgow policemen was despatched to quell the riot that had developed and they fought a battle with the crofters. Later gunboats were sent and marines landed at Uig.

The result of this was a Royal Commission, set up by Gladstone, to investigate the crofters' grievances, and in 1886 the Crofters Act was passed, giving security of tenure at a fair rent. The present-day crofter usually has a full-time job or a pension, using his land to supplement his livelihood.

The sheep kept on the island are mainly Scottish blackface, an exceptionally hardy breed, and cheviots. Cattle are also kept, mainly for beef, and many of these are exported each year. The Forestry Commission has over 8000 acres of trees; there is little natural woodland.

A small inshore fishing fleet operates around the island catching prawns for export to France and Italy and some white fish, which is sent to Aberdeen. Other shellfish, including scallops, are also taken.

It is tourism that has brought a measure of prosperity to the island, but even this has its drawbacks. The demand for holiday homes has pushed property prices beyond the reach of indigenous young married couples, and not enough jobs have been created to stem the flow of emigration. The

high cost of living, due to transport costs, coupled with a lack of job opportunities, provides little incentive to stay.

In AD 585 St Columba visited Skye, and later Maolrubha became the patron saint of the central and southern areas – in the past, 25 August was celebrated in Broadford as his feast day. In the 8thC, Norsemen began raiding, and finally settled; their domination of Skye, under the Kingdom of Man and the Isles, lasted until three years after the Battle of Largs in 1263, when King Haakon of Norway was defeated. A legacy of Norse blood and place-names remains strong on the island.

John MacDonald of Islay, a descendant of Somerled (who split the Kingdom of Man and the Isles in 1158), first adopted the title Lord of the Isles, with Skye as an administrative centre; the title lasted until 1748. The land was divided between the MacDonalds and the MacLeods, and the sites of their battles on the island are a reminder of their constant feuds. The inhabitants professed Catholicism until the Reformation in 1561; Evangelism spread from 1805, followed by the Free Church from 1843, with its dour teachings. In common with other Protestant western islands, Sunday is observed as the Lord's Day. Shops, pubs and restaurants close, and no work, unless absolutely essential, is done. There are those who will not listen to the radio, watch television, read a newspaper or even light a fire on a Sunday – but the influence of hundreds of thousands of visitors to the island has generally made for a slightly more relaxed approach here than on, say, Lewis in the Outer Hebrides. The Gaelic language is spoken, but most young people now use English.

Skye people once had a reputation for second sight: seeing a person in a shroud prophesied death; seeing a fire spark fall on someone's arm signified they would soon carry a dead child. The other people on the island were the fairies, or *sithche* (pronounced sheeche) – from *sithchean* (the noiseless people) – who lived in any rounded grassy mound (a *sithein*, pronounced shi-en) and performed miraculous or mischievous deeds. If you wanted protection from these small people, you carried iron, steel or oatmeal.

The story of one of Scotland's most popular and heroic partnerships unfolded on Skye. In 1745 Prince Charles Edward Stuart, Bonnie Prince Charlie, came to Scotland to attempt to depose George II and regain the crown of England for the Stuarts. After gathering together a small army, the Young Pretender enjoyed some initial success, but was finally routed at Culloden and his Jacobite army dispersed. Pursued by the King's forces, with a price of £30,000 on his head, he fled to the islands from whence he hoped to escape to Scandinavia or France. Disguised as Betty Burke, a maid, he was brought from Benbecula to Kilbride Bay in Trotternish by Flora MacDonald, a 24-year-old Edinburgh-educated Skye girl. After some close escapes, hiding in caves and cattle byres, he left Flora and went to Raasay the night after it had been sacked by troops from the Royal Navy ship *Furnace* as retribution against the men of the island who had supported the Jacobites. After a short stay, waiting for a French ship which never appeared, he went back to Skye, then on to Knoydart on the mainland. Finally, on 19 September 1746 a French ship took him from Loch nam Uamh, and he died in Rome in 1778. Flora was arrested after his escape and held prisoner in a private house in London, but she was freed after the passing of the Indemnity Act in 1747, when she became the heroine of London society. Her grave and monument are in a simple burial ground in Kilmuir.

The bare rocks and peaks of the Cuillins and Trotternish and the sea cliffs around Dunvegan Head and Loch Harport are the habitat of the island's golden eagles. Sea birds and waterfowl inhabit the lochs, and many of these are fished for brown trout; the rivers run with sea trout and salmon, although these have declined due to over-

The museum at Luib, Skye

The Storr and the Old Man of Storr, Skye

fishing at sea.

The richness of the island's flora was shown in a detailed study which revealed 589 species of flowering plants and ferns, 370 mosses, 181 liverworts and 154 lichens. Many alpines are to be found on the eastern side of the Trotternish ridge, including the tiny Iceland-purslane (*Koenigia islandica*), a relative of the sorrels, first discovered here in 1934. In the limestone crossing Strath Suardal behind Broadford, there is a birchwood where mountain avens, guelderrose and helleborine grow. The rare red broomrape is found on grassy slopes above the sea, and rock whitebeam occurs on some of the low cliffs.

The largest wild mammal in Britain, the red deer, is found mostly around Loch Coruisk and in Sleat. Whales are sometimes seen off the coast, usually the herring whale (common rorqual), but killer whales have also been seen chasing seals.

Portree and Trotternish

The only town on Skye is Portree. The name is anglicised from *Port en Righ*, Port of the King, so called in honour of a visit by James V in the 16thC. Prior to this it was called Kiltragleann, the church at the foot of the glen. It is attractively sited with a fine sheltered anchorage, but apart from the usual services of a town – shops, hotels, library, schools, police station – there is little of architectural or historic interest, although McNab's Inn, once the Royal Hotel, does have associations with Bonnie Prince Charlie and Flora MacDonald (the room in which he bade her farewell is here). The tourist office is situated in the building that was once both courthouse and jail for the whole island; the present courthouse in Somerled Square was built in 1867. In the cliffs to the north of Loch Portree is Mac Coitir's Cave, said to run beneath the island to Bracadale. Portree is the natural centre for touring the Trotternish, Waternish and Duirinish peninsulas and much of the centre of the island.

The coast road north of Portree to Trotternish is dominated by The Storr (2358 ft) and the Old Man of Storr, a rock needle 165-ft tall, precariously balanced among sheer cliffs and many smaller pinnacles, which was first climbed in 1955. The name Storr is from *fiacaill storàch*, meaning buck tooth. Here the ground is loose and treacherous and should be treated with caution. Below are Lochs Fada and Leathan, the reservoir for the Hydro which has supplied the island's electricity since 1952 (there is also an electric cable across the Kyle of Lochalsh). Before 1949 the only electricity was generated by a diesel engine belonging to the Portree Hotel.

In the cliffs east of Loch Fada is the cave where Bonnie Prince Charlie landed on his return from Raasay, and at Lealt there are spectacular waterfalls which can be seen by taking a not too difficult climb down the ravine. Three-quarters of a mile south, on the shore, is Eaglais Bhreagach, a church-shaped rock where the Clan MacQueen is said to have raised the devil, using an ancient ceremony called *Taghairm*, involving the roasting of live cats.

At Lonfearn the remains of beehive dwellings (early Christian circular stone cells) were discovered – in Gaelic they are called *tighean nan druineach*, druids' houses. To the west, on the Trotternish ridge, can be seen the summit of Beinn Edra (2003 ft); in the spring of 1945 a Flying Fortress bomber hit it in the midday mist – all on board were killed. Up the coast again there is a simple black-house museum at Elishader, and in the cliffs nearby can be seen the kilt rock, black basalt so called because of the folds and pattern of its strata.

A galleon of the Spanish Armada was reputed to have been wrecked near Staffin, some coins having been found, and there are people here said to be of Spanish descent. These crofting townships are overlooked by the fantastic Quiraing (round fold) – awesome rock formations where whole herds of cattle could be hidden. The Table, the 120-ft-tall Needle and the Prison can all be explored by walking north from the Staffin-to-Uig road near its highest point.

In the bay below, a road signposted Staffin Slip leads to some areas of dark sand among boulders, facing the low-lying **Staffin Island**, with its grazing sheep and bothy used by fishermen. **Eilean Flodigarry**, rising to a steep point at its eastern tip, once (according to legend) had its corn reaped in two nights by seven score and ten fairies. When they had finished, they asked for more work, so the owner set them to empty the sea! Behind the bay, the crofting land can be seen clearly divided into regular strips.

To the north of the Quiraing is the Flodigarry Hotel, a turreted building, once the home of Flora MacDonald after her escapades with the Prince. North of The Aird lies the grassy **Eilean Trodday**, the trolls isle, which once supported a herd of dairy cattle. This northern end of Trotternish was known as the granary of Skye due to its fertile basaltic soil.

As the road reaches the west coast the few craggy remains of Duntulm Castle can be seen at the top of a steep cliff, above the hotel. The main part of the castle is 15thC (it was occupied up to 1732), and a footpath from the road leads to the ruin. In the bay lies **Tulm Island**, a narrow green hump, and about three miles north-west are the flat-topped **Lord Macdonald's Table, Gearran Island, Gaeilavore Island** and the largest of the group, **Fladda-chùain** with its ruined chapel dedicated to St Columba, the blue altar stone said to bring fair winds to becalmed fishermen. Sir Donald MacDonald of the Isles is supposed to have hidden title deeds here before taking part in the Rising of 1715.

The Skye Cottage Museum at Kilmuir consists of four restored black houses on an exposed site overlooking the sea, with typi-cal room settings and a peat fire, Bonnie Prince Charlie and Flora MacDonald relics and a particularly interesting collection of historical documents relating to life on the islands. Nearby in a small graveyard is the new memorial to Flora MacDonald; the original MacDonald mausoleum was gradually taken, piece by piece, by tourists. Close to this is a well-preserved crusader slab.

Between Balgown and the coast lies an area of marshy ground, which was once Loch Chaluim Chille. Drained in 1824, on what were once islands are the remains of beehive dwellings. From the main road at Linicro a very rough track leads to the ruins of Sir Alexander MacDonald's once-fine house, Monkstadt. Flora and the Prince landed at Kilbride Bay and came to the house, only to find it occupied by the King's officers; the pair then fled through Kingsburgh to Portree.

The road descends steeply to the very pretty township of Uig (bay or nook), sheltered by steep basaltic cliffs, its scattered crofts stretching back to the hills where there is, along Glen Uig to Balnacnock, a Quiraing in miniature. The round tower opposite the Uig pier is a folly built by Captain Fraser. There is also a youth hostel here.

At the head of Loch Snizort Beag, on the eastern side, stands Caisteal Uisdein (Hugh's castle) built around 1580 by Hugh MacDonald of Sleat, who schemed against his chief and died entombed in Duntulm Castle with a piece of salt beef and an empty water jug. A farm track north of Hinnisdal Bridge leads towards the ruin.

The central region of the Trotternish peninsula is wild, inhospitable, heather-clad country with steep cliffs and peat bogs.

Loch Snizort Beag and Waternish

The road from Portree to the Waternish peninsula passes through a broad valley at the head of Loch Snizort Beag. On an islet in the River Snizort are the scant ruins of a chapel associated with St Columba, best seen from the old bridge by Skeabost post office (a path and stepping stones lead to the ruin), and the Skeabost Hotel, an imposing white castellated building. The village itself is notable as the birthplace of the poet, Mary MacPherson. On a hill above Clachamish stand the remains of Dùn Suladale, one of the best preserved of the 20 brochs on the island, many of which are now reduced to barely recognisable heaps of stones.

The road then passes Edinbane, where there is a pottery, and on through peaty moorland to the Fairy Bridge with its legendary associations with the MacLeods of Dunvegan. As you head north along the Waternish peninsula, the village of Stein is reached, nestling on the east side of Loch Bay, backed by crofts and looking out towards the cliffs of Beinn Bhreac, and the low-lying islands of **Isay, Mingay** and **Clett**,

once inhabited, but cleared in 1860. Isay
was offered to Dr Johnson by the MacLeods,
on condition that he built a house on it, but,
needless to say, such a comfort-lover did not
accept the offer. Stein has a hotel, an attractive terrace, a fine stone house and a small
jetty by a stony beach. In 1787 a fishing
industry was started here, but the project
was abandoned in 1837. Above Hallin the
remains of a broch can be seen, the walls
standing about seven-feet high in places. To
the east is Gillen, where there is a knitting
workshop, and fine views of the uninhabited **Ascrib Islands**, where a colony of puffins have burrowed into the basalt. Stone for
Caisteal Uisdein is said to have been quarried there.

At the end of the road, above Ardmore
Bay, stands the lonely and windswept ruin
of Trumpan Church. It was here in 1578 that
the MacDonalds of Uist barred the door on a
congregation of MacLeods, and set fire to the
church, to avenge the Eigg massacre (see
Eigg). The only survivor in 1578, a girl,
escaped by a window, severing one of her
breasts as she squeezed through to raise the
alarm. Other MacLeods arrived, carrying
their legendary Fairy Flag, just in time to
capture the MacDonald galleys, slaughter-
ing all on board. The bodies were buried in
a dyke; hence the battle is known as the
spoiling of the dyke.

In the churchyard are some ancient
graves, including that of Lady Grange, who
was exiled on St Kilda for eight years by her
husband, and died three years after her
return in 1742. A track near the church leads
north towards Waternish Point.

Dunvegan and Duirinish
One mile north of the Fairy Bridge is Annait
where there are remains of some early Christian cells. From the bridge the road continues south to Dunvegan, with its hotels,
shops, boat trips to see the seals, and Dunvegan Castle, seat of the Clan MacLeod since
1200 – no other Scottish castle has been con-
tinuously occupied as long. The first building on the site is said to date from the 9thC,
but the major part of the present one is
19thC, beautifully situated at the head of
Loch Dunvegan and backed by mixed woodland planted since 1890. The castle contains
many MacLeod relics including the 15thC
Dunvegan Cup, Rory Mor's drinking horn
and the legendary Fairy Flag (*Bratach shith
MhicLèoid*), made of yellow silk from the
Near East. Its miraculous saving powers can
only be used three times, when the survival
of the clan is threatened; there is now only
one more opportunity left. Pregnant women
should also take into consideration the
myth that, upon seeing the flag, they may go
into premature labour. The castle is closed
from mid-October to March.

To the north is Claigan, where a signposted track leads down to the coral beaches

Dunvegan Castle, Skye

– the first a small rocky bay, then on to a
more dramatic sweep. Up a track behind
Claigan Farm, the entrance to a souterrain
(an Iron Age or earlier earth house or food
store) can be found. There is another example near Loch Duagrich, to the east of
Bracadale.

Duirinish is dominated by the twin flat
peaks of Healabhal Bheag (1601 ft) and
Healabhal Mhor (1538 ft) – MacLeod's
Tables. It is an area of wild moorland, with
the few roads keeping to the coast – the
southern part is accessible only on foot. The
main road rounds the head of Loch Dunvegan; a narrow track leads south to Orbost
where a small art gallery has been established. From here, another track leads down
to a small sheltered beach.

By heading north-west along the side of
Loch Dunvegan, containing low-lying
islands grazed by sheep, the tiny village of
Colbost, with its Black House Museum and
Three Chimneys restaurant, is reached.
Behind the museum, which depicts life
around 100 years ago, is a replica of an illicit
whisky still.

To the north, past Husabost, is Bor
reraig, where the legendary MacCrimmons,
hereditary pipers to the MacLeod chiefs
from 1500 to 1800, are said to have established their piping college. They were the
first composers, players and teachers of *pib-
roch* (a tune with variations), and their history and folklore is recorded in the museum,
founded in 1975 in the unimposing cream
house to the west of the road. On the promontory opposite, above the supposed
remains of the original college, stands the
beehive-shaped MacCrimmon Memorial
Cairn, the focal point of an annual pilgrim-
age of MacCrimmons, and in the cliffs below
is the Piper's Cave. The first piping school
on Skye was established by the MacArthurs,
who later went to Islay as hereditary pipers
to the Lords of the Isles.

The main road from Colbost to Glendale
passes the memorial to the Glendale Land
Leaguers, 600 crofters who challenged Government forces and now own the Glendale
Estate. The township of Glendale stretches

back along the river valley behind Loch Pooltiel, where the hills to the west slope gently away and the scattered crofts are well tended and productive. Below the low cliffs at the water's edge is the Glendale Water Mill, a 200-year-old dry-stone grain mill with a thatched roof. It ceased operation in 1914, but was restored in 1971-72 to virtually its original working condition, the project being carried out on local initiative using local skills. Unfortunately the mill burned down in 1973, on the day the Skeabost mill stones were brought here: in legend, whenever these stones are moved, there is a disaster. The second restoration started immediately, and the mill now sells handmade oiled woollen knitwear and tweed. Close by stands a dry-stone kiln, where peat was burned to dry grain before milling. There is a spectacular waterfall tumbling down the cliffs opposite.

The most westerly point on Skye is the sheer-sided and narrow Neist peninsula, where the well-made but steep path to the lighthouse makes a good walk. There are some accessible small bays, towering cliffs with sea birds, and superb views of Waterstein Head, 967-ft high. On a clear day, North and South Uist and Benbecula can be seen, low on the horizon.

A narrow and bumpy road across rugged moorland and peat bogs leads to Ramasaig, an isolated settlement, from which a track goes to Lorgill, the glen of the deer's cry. In 1830 all ten crofting families there were ordered to Loch Snizort to either board the *Midlothian* bound for Nova Scotia, or go to prison, and those over 70 years of age were to be sent to the county poorhouse. On 4 August that year, they all left. Idrigill Point can be reached on foot, but it is stiff walking.

Bracadale and Minginish

The south of Duirinish shelters Loch Bracadale, with its calm inlets and small islands, tiered cliffs and irregular hills. It is a magical part of the island, especially at sunset on a fine day, when the Cuillins are etched with deep shadows, and the sea glows between the headlands.

Above the township of Struan is Dùn Beag, the best-preserved broch on Skye – parts of the galleries may still be seen. Bracadale, established in 1772 by Thomas Pennant, stands at the head of Loch Beag, scattered crofts above a small beach. The view towards the lighthouse at Ardtreck Point and Portnalong is splendid.

The main road to Sligachan passes through Glen Drynoch. At the head of Loch Harport a minor road crosses the River Drynoch and continues along the west side of the loch, passing the Talisker Malt Whisky Distillery at Carbost. Originally founded by Kenneth MacAskill of Talisker House at Snizort, it was first moved to Fis-

kavaig, then finally to Carbost in 1830. Talisker Whisky can be tasted in most of the hotels and bars on the island, and bottles are widely available. There are conducted tours in the summer but, alas, no free samples. The road behind the distillery leads to Talisker Bay, reached through a steep-sided glen, where cattle and sheep graze, and crops grow on the fertile plain. In the cliffs to the north a fine waterfall spills to the sea, and a footpath leads to a secluded beach with views of the Outer Hebrides.

To the south, at the head of the loch, is Eynort, with its wooden houses among conifer plantations, behind a sheltered beach. Further north along Loch Harport, the road finishes by the pier and sheltered small boat anchorage of Portnalong, a township of crofters from Lewis and Harris who came here in 1921. To the west is Fiskavaig, a crofting township above a stony bay, and to the north-west, across the mouth of Loch Bracadale, the three basaltic stacks of MacLeod's Maidens can be seen just off Idrigill Point, named after a MacLeod chief's wife and daughters who drowned near here. The views of the Cuillins from Loch Harport are dramatic, the stark black gabbro contrasting with the softer crofting land at the head of the loch.

From Carbost, a narrow road leads south between the Cuillins and the Glen Brittle Forest, ending by the sandy beach at Loch Brittle where, in summer, the campsite is full of the brightly-coloured tents of climbers tackling the sharp peaks, the surfaces of which appear barren and lunar – land stripped to the bone, beautiful and cruel. The rock is hard, making for some of the best climbing in the country. Those who do not climb can stare in wonder at the tiny figures traversing and ascending the steep slopes. Those who do climb (or walk up) are rewarded with a staggering panorama of the Hebrides, as distant as St Kilda. There are paths to the top (the summit with the best access for walkers is Sgurr Alasdair via Coire Làgan, also Bruach na Frithe via the north-west ridge from Sligachan), but it must be remembered that this is no place to get stranded in mist or a squall without proper equipment and experience – the mountains do not forgive your mistakes. A Forestry Commission picnic site halfway along the glen overlooks Coire na Creiche, the scene of the last battle between the MacDonalds and the MacLeods.

Central Skye

South of Portree the road to Sligachan passes through Glen Varragill – unremarkable apart from good views of the Cuillins at the southern end. To the east lie The Braes, scene of a fight between crofters denied grazing rights and an expeditionary force of Glasgow policemen on 19 April 1882. This melée is sometimes referred to as the last

Uig, Skye

battle on British soil. A small cairn by the roadside commemorates this battle fought on behalf of the crofters of Gaeldom. This road finished at Peinchorran: along its length are a few crofts where once there were many, and ruined black houses now stand beside the worst sort of modern chalet bungalows, yet the feeling is of peace, and the views of Raasay are good.

The old hotel at Sligachan, beautifully situated at the head of the loch with a mountain backdrop, was once a climbing centre for the Cuillins. From the bridge, as you look south along Glen Sligachan, the difference between the gabbro to the west, spiky and angular, and the granite to the east, smoothed by erosion, can be clearly seen. A track through the glen leads to the isolated and dramatic glacial basin of Loch Coruisk (*coire uish*, the cauldron of water) at the head of Loch Scavaig. Loch Coruisk remains little changed since the thawing of the ice that scooped it out 100-ft deeper than the water of Loch Scavaig – a primeval, lonely place. At the seaward end of Loch Sligachan is Sconser, the ferry terminal for Raasay and site of the island's main nine-hole golf course. Of the two routes to Loch Ainort, the minor road by the coast is more pleasant.

On the southern shore of the loch is Luib, with its folk museum, a black house restored in 1978 by the energetic Peter MacAskill who has been responsible for saving other similar buildings on the island. There are room settings, showing interiors of about 50 years ago, a peat fire burning in

the stove and some farm implements. During restoration two guns, dating from the 1745 rising, were found hidden under the roof. Outside roam a small flock of blackface tups, sheep noted for their longevity.

Beyond the forestry plantations is Broadford, a formless village that serves as the main centre for the south of the island. There is little of interest, but all main services – shops, hotels, bed-and-breakfasts, bank, post office, garage, youth hostel and tourist information – are available. The beach is untidy stone and shingle, and at one time the steamer used to call here on the way to Portree. The village is dominated by Bienn na Callich (2403 ft), on the top of which is a large and conspicuous cairn with, reputedly, a Norwegian princess buried beneath. The walk to the summit is not difficult and the views of Skye and Walter Ross are just reward.

Across Broadford Bay can be seen **Pabay** (priest or monk island – 350 acres) noted for its limestone fossils and past associations with pirates. Licensed to produce postage stamps, it has a ruined chapel, a burial ground and two houses. It was described in the 1500s as being 'full of woods, good for fishing, and a main shelter for thieves and cut-throats'. To the north east is **Scalpay**, rough and heather-clad, rising to 1298 ft at the summit of Mullach na Càrn, although the area around Scalpay House, in the south-east corner behind a small tidal harbour, is cultivated. There are several lochs and many streams, and large areas of conifers have been planted. 4000 acres on the north-west side are fenced for intensive deer farming.

The island was first developed in the 19thC by Sir Donald Currie who made roads and planted trees; it is now owned by a merchant banker and worked by his sons.

To the west of Scalpay House are the remains of a chapel, built on the site of a Celtic cell. Opposite Ard Dorch on the east coast of Skye, a cottage is let for holidays. At low tide the island seems almost to join Skye at Caolas Scalpay. To the east is **Longay**, rising to 221 ft at the southern end of a reef running parallel to Scalpay; to the south is the small low-lying **Guillamon Island.**

Waterloo is the eastward continuation of Broadford; in 1815, over 1500 Skye men fought at the Battle of Waterloo and, on return, many veterans made their home here. Behind Broadford the road to Elgol passes along Strath Suardal, a wide valley to the south of Bienn na Caillich. Below here, at Coire-chatachan, are the ruins of the house where Mackinnon entertained Boswell and Johnson during their tour of the Hebrides in 1773. By the road on a small rise is the ancient graveyard and crumbling walls of Cill Chriosd, where St Maolrubha founded a church in the 7thC – the last service was held in the mid-19thC.

As you approach Torrin, by Loch Slapin, there is a marble quarry, its spoil heaps gleaming white, and nearby a track leads to a small beach. To the south, a few ruined walls are all that remain of Suisnish, a once thriving crofting community that was cleared to Canada. Over the loch the bare rock, deep crevices and scree of Blà Bheinn (3044 ft) contrast dramatically with the gentle shoreline. Kilmarie, on the east of Strathiard, was once the home of the Mackinnon chiefs. From the main road, a well-signposted track leads west to the fine isolated beach at Camasunary and on over the bridge to Loch Coruisk, this walk made difficult by The Bad Step, a rock obstacle.

The main road ends at Elgol, passing a thriving area of crofts before descending steeply to the stone and shingle beach and jetty. Virtually on the beach is the school – a marvellous, if somewhat exposed, position, where the view across Loch Scavaig to the Cuillins is particularly good. At Suidhe Biorach, half a mile to the south, is the cave where Bonnie Prince Charlie was hidden before leaving Skye – childless women were supposed to become fertile after sitting on this promontory.

A narrow and winding road crosses the peninsula to Glasnakille, a village of crofts along a steep and mainly inaccessible shore; the Spar Cave, best explored at low tide with a torch, contains stalactites. A track leads down to a deep gash in the cliffs; the path along the top affords fine views of Sleat.

Sleat

The road from Broadford to Sleat passes a low-lying area. A smaller road west of the main one leads to Drumfearn, a pretty crofting township where a track leads down to the sheltered rocky head of Loch Eishort, with small fishing boats, and cattle and sheep grazing by the shore. The main road and the main centres of population are on the fertile eastern side of the peninsula, the garden of Skye, with woodland, forest plantations, crofts and farms, and a mainly rocky shore. At the southern end of Loch na Dal is Isleornsay, a very pretty village with a pier, rusting anchors and chains, and small moored boats. The small tidal island of **Ornsay**, to which you can cross at low tide, has a ruined chapel and an unmanned lighthouse, built in 1857. There is an attractive beach at Camascross to the south. The road rejoins the coast at Teangue, where the ivy-clad ruins of Knock Castle, built in the 14thC, stand at the edge of a small bay, many of its stones having been taken to build Knock House.

A Gaelic college has been established in the restored farm at Ostaig, part of a large estate owned by an Edinburgh merchant banker who has successfully revitalised this part of the island. Gaelic language courses are held in the summer, with piping courses in the spring and autumn, and there is a bookshop selling Gaelic books and souvenirs.

Armadale Castle, designed by Gillespie Graham and built 1815-19 for the second Lord MacDonald, stands above the road in fine grounds planted with North American hardwoods, conifers and Australasian and European trees. The castle is now the Clan Donald Centre (there are estimated to be three million MacDonalds, dispersed throughout the world), with a display of relics, crafts and books, and a restaurant. The pier to the south is the terminal for the Mallaig ferry, and provides shelter for the Skye Yacht Club moorings. South of Ardvasar the road narrows and becomes quite dramatic, with fine views of Knoydart, Morar and Moidart and ending at the crofting township of Aird of Sleat where a track, impassable for cars, continues to the lighthouse at the Point of Sleat, the extreme southern tip of Skye, looking out towards Rum, Eigg and Ardnamurchan.

On the west of Sleat there are three settlements reached by a narrow scenic road through low irregular hills, in a loop from Knock to Ostaig. The most northerly of these habitations is Ord, where there is a hotel above a small bay of pebbles and a little sand. Further south is Tokavaig, with crofts, and the remains of Dunscaith Castle built into the rock and overlooking the bay, a stronghold of the MacDonalds during the 15th and 16thC, and in legend occupied by

The lighthouse island of Ornsay, Skye

the Queen of Skye, who taught the art of war to Cuchulainn, an Irish hero. It is one of the oldest fortified headlands in the Hebrides and was last occupied around 1570; access to it is difficult. The largest of the three communities is Tarskavaig, with crofts to the north of a small beach with sand at low tide, and rocks and skerries out to sea. This isolated area of western Sleat is well worth visiting. It has great intrinsic beauty, and a superb view of the jagged peaks of the Cuillins, cloud-topped in a sweep above Coruisk.

Eastern Skye and the Kyles

Skye's most ancient ferry terminal is at Kylerhea, a small township overlooking Kyle Rhea. As recently as 1906, cattle were swum across the narrows to the mainland at slack water, tied nose to tail in strings of six or eight behind a boat – up to 8000 head a year were once taken off the island in this way. It is now the terminal for the Glenelg ferry, linked to the main Broadford to Kyleakin road by the steep and narrow pass through Glen Arroch, with its summit at 911 ft.

Kyleakin was once a fishing village, but it is now the main ferry terminal for Skye with a continous seven-day-a-week service. The Sunday service was started in 1965 against a background of strong protest, led by Rev. Angus Smith, Free Church minister for Skeabost, who also instigated the narrowly defeated anti-alcohol poll two years later. The village overlooks the swift-flowing waters of Kyle Akin, where King Haakon moored in 1263 on his way to defeat at the Battle of Largs. The entrance to the harbour is guarded by the ruins of Caisteal Maol, used by the Mackinnons from the 12th to the

15thC. Apparently a Norwegian princess, resident in an earlier building on this site, stretched a chain across the Kyle to extract tolls from passing ships – an imaginative legend and an equally imaginative piece of engineering! The village has shops, hotels, restaurants and other services, and there are boat trips from here in the summer.

Four miles to the west of Kyleakin is the Skye airstrip, used by Loganair and Bristow Helicopters who have a new geodesic hangar. Near here, where a stream crosses the shore, is the spot where St Maolrubha preached – keeping his scriptures in the rocks and hanging a bell from the branches of a tree. A graveyard at the end of the runway overlooks many small islands and skerries where cattle are sometimes stranded by the tide. A neat row of graves stands as a reminder of the sinking of the cruiser, *HMS Curaçao*, cut in two by the liner, *Queen Mary*, while acting as her escort on 2 October 1942. The scattered crofts of Upper and Lower Breakish (the name said to derive from *a'bhreac*, smallpox, that swept through the island in the 17th and 18thC) are of little interest, but the old schoolhouse on the main road is the office of the *West Highland Free Press*, a controversial campaigning newspaper started in 1972, and distributed throughout the isles.

Skye's close proximity to the mainland makes for easy and inexpensive access. The main Caledonian MacBrayne vehicle ferries *Kyleakin* and *Lochalsh* operate virtually non-stop, from morning to night, seven days a week, from the railhead at Kyle of Lochalsh to Kyleakin: a five-minute passage. A Monday to Saturday ferry service is operated in the summer between Glenelg and Kylerhea, carrying vehicles up to four tons: also a five-minute passage. Another Monday to Saturday, summer-only vehicle ferry is operated by Caledonian Mac-Brayne's *Iona* between Mallaig (a railhead) and Armadale: a 30 minute passage. During the winter this service is for passengers only, and is provided by Caledonian MacBrayne's *Lochmor*.

Ferries operate from Sconser to Raasay, and from Uig to the Outer Hebrides, both carrying vehicles.

The main Tourist Information Centre is in Portree, with a smaller seasonal office in Broadford.

Raasay

Highland. With a population of 150, Raasay is 13 miles long by 3 miles wide, rising to a height of 1456 ft at the distinctive flat-topped summit of Dùn Caan upon which the ebullient Dr Johnson danced a reel.

The north of the island is composed of Archaean gneiss, the south being Torridonian sandstone with two large areas of granite. Some of the Torridonian shales contain the oldest plant remains yet discovered. A feature almost unique in the Highlands is the strong loam present between 600 and 900 ft at The Glam. The presence of this soil suggests that Raasay probably escaped glaciation leaving much ancient and rare flora on the east coast. The disused mineworkings in the south are evidence of ironstone deposits, no longer of economic use.

The present ferry service between Sconser and Suisnish, started by Caledonian MacBrayne in July 1976 after a long campaign by the islanders, helped to stem the island's declining fortunes. Although there is full employment many of the people are elderly, and the boarding out in Portree of children over 11 years of age during the school term does little to encourage them to stay in later years.

Raasay was once the centre of a breakaway section of the Free Church, formed in 1893 by a Mr MacFarlane, with an even more uncompromising doctrine than the original. All pleasure was suspect: music, dancing and poetry, once strong on the island, were banned. Today the original Free Church on the island has a few supporters, but most people belong to the church of the breakaway group, and this plays an important part in the island's life. The Sabbath is therefore strictly observed – no work, no play, and people going out only to church. The community is a caring one, sharing fortune and misfortune alike, and the people are happy to receive visitors – as long as their ways are respected.

Inverarish is the main village, with a fine general store, a post office, and terraced houses built by Baird & Co. for their mineworkers. Above the village are the remains of Dùn Borodale, a broch with parts of the walls and galleries remaining.

Behind Inverarish the road passes through the forest and the disused mineworkings where German POWs worked during World War I, and on to North and South Fearns, four restored cottages where, in 1919, families from Rona (the Rona Raiders) seized the land from Baird's. The men were put on trial amid a public outcry, but were subsequently released and piped triumphantly home. The view from

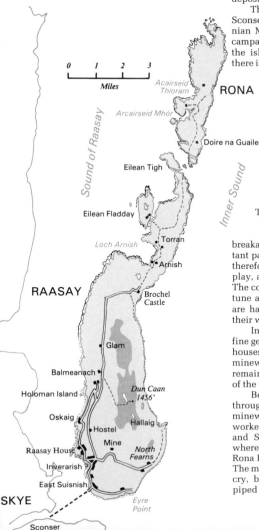

Raasay House

here towards the Kyle is of immense beauty – layer upon layer of mountains in receding colours, often set against vast cloud formations swept in from the Atlantic. A path leads north from the Fearns to the waterfall by the shore at Hallaig.

On the north side of Churchton Bay stands Raasay House, a fine building backed by mixed woodland. It stands on the site of a tower built in 1549, which was replaced with a house subsequently burned down (along with all the cottages on the island) during the reprisals after the Rising of 1745. Raasay and Rona supported the Prince, and both paid dearly for it. This ancestral home of the MacLeods was again rebuilt, and was visited by Johnson and Boswell in 1773 during their tour of the Hebrides. They were suitably entertained with food and music: 'I know not how we shall get away,' said Johnson, in his contentment.

James MacLeod improved the estate during the early 1800s and added the Regency frontage to the house.

The population on the island grew rapidly, poverty became widespread, and emigration began. In 1843, due to heavy debt, John MacLeod was forced to sell the island. The purchaser was George Rainy of Edinburgh, who paid 35,000 guineas (£36,750). Taking possession in 1846 after the last of the MacLeods had emigrated to Australia, Rainy genuinely tried to improve conditions on Raasay, but without success – so he turned to sheep farming and evicted over 100 families. On his death in 1863, ownership passed to his son, who before his premature death in 1872, aged 27, used the island as a holiday retreat.

Raasay then had several owners, each with little sympathy for the crofters, until Baird's bought it in 1912 to extract the iron-ore; the mine was worked from 1913 to 1919. The present owners of the island, the Scottish Department of Agriculture and Fisheries, bought it for £37,000 in 1922, following the exploits of the Rona Raiders.

Raasay House was run as a hotel from 1937 to 1960, after which a doctor from Sussex bought it, together with the Home Farm and various other buildings. He allowed the house, its contents, and the garden to fall into decay, as well as refusing to sell the more suitable pier at Clachan for use as a terminal for the badly-needed ferry. All this echoed the attitudes of the absentee landlords of the last century. After years of uncertainty, Raasay House was finally sold, in a sorry and delapidated state, but now seems to be thriving as an outdoor centre. Borodale House is now a hotel.

The narrow road north passes by the stables and beneath the clocktower where 36 men of Raasay assembled in 1914 to go to war. The clock stopped as they left and, despite many attempts at repair, has never been restarted: it was an ill omen – only 14 men returned and they found the island in a very poor state. Behind the house stand the ruins of the 13thC chapel dedicated to St Moluag on an ancient burial ground with two other buildings, the smaller of which possible dates from the 11thC. One of the gravestones records the drowning off Rona in 1880 of Murdoch and Roderich MacLeod, brothers aged 26 and 24.

Beyond here, at the start of the signposted Temptation Hill, by a fuchsia hedge, stands an incised Pictish symbol stone, perhaps dating from the 7thC; another similar design is carved into a rock near the Battery, a small defensive structure built in 1807 in front of Raasay House, armed with cannon and two less-than-beautiful mermaids. These incised stones may have been part of a series marking an area of sanctuary.

The road winds around Balmeanach, with its crofts and a loch nestling in a sheltered valley. A path south-east to the summit of Dùn Caan leaves the road near here; the view from the flat top is magnificent. To the south of the mountains is Loch na Mna, the woman's loch, so named because a water-horse haunting it abducted a woman; the local smithy killed the monster, finding it to be made of jelly. To the west is Loch Storab, taking its name from the nearby grave of a Norwegian prince.

The Fearns, Raasay

The tarmac road ends at the scant remains of Brochel Casle, probably built by the MacLeods of Lewis in the 15thC, from which they raided ships in the Inner Sound, attracting many lawless men into the Clan. Iain Garbh was the last MacLeod chief to live here dying in 1671. One-and-a-half miles south, on the coast, are the remains of the township of South Screapadal, nestling in a steep valley. It is a good two-and-a-half hour walk from here through broken, rocky, heather-clad ground to Caol Rona. The first two miles of road were built single-handedly with pick, shovel and wheelbarrow by Calum MacLeod, one of the island's most northerly inhabitants, to his home at Arnish. Through Torran, where the post office and school closed in 1960, **Eilean Fladday** is reached, where there were once four families with their own school, but now all the cottages are holiday homes. The island can be reached on foot at low tide. Off the north tip of Raasay is **Eilean Tigh**; at low tide, a rock ledge, joining it to Raasay and wide enough to walk across, is uncovered. The rough, rocky country here is the haunt of golden eagle.

The plant life on the island is particularly rich, with many ancient and rare plants making the island a venue for botanists. You can expect to find many alpines, saxifrages, ferns and mosses; also orchids, sea aster and bog asphodel. Mammals include red deer, otter, alpine hare, water shrew and a species of bankvole, with a skull slightly larger than normal, unique to Raasay.

The only means of transport to the island is the Caledonian MacBrayne vehicle ferry *Raasay* from Sconser on Skye. There are up to five daily return journeys, Monday to Saturday, 15-minute crossing. There is no petrol for sale on the island.

Island of Rona

Highland. Often known as South Rona, this is the northerly continuation of Raasay, separated from it by the half-mile channel of Caol Rona. Five miles long by about one-and-a-half miles wide, rising to 404ft at the centre, Rona is composed of Archaean gneiss. Its only inhabitants, apart from the seals and birds, are the Royal Navy personnel who man the Nato signal station at the far northern tip. The lighthouse is now automatic.

At one time there were three settlements, two schools and a church. During the 16thC, the island, then thickly wooded, was the retreat of robbers and pirates who raided shipping from the fine natural harbour of Acairseid Mhór – known at the time as *Port nan Robaireann*, the Port of Robbers.

The island belonged to the MacLeods of Raasay until the time of the Clearances, when crofters evicted from Raasay settled at Doire na Guaile, Acairseid Mhór (big harbour) and Acairseid Thioram (dry harbour), breaking the barren ground with picks and fertilising it with seaweed. In the mid-19thC there were 150 head of cattle kept on Rona in spite of the poor soil; now only sheep graze, tended from Skye.

By the end of World War I, Rona, like Raasay, was in a poor economic state and no Government help was made available to the crofters. In 1919 a group of seven families seized fertile land at Eyre and North and South Fearns on Raasay, rowing across Caol Rona with their sheep and 20 cattle; soon there was only one family on Rona who also subsequently left. The overgrown remains of the three settlements can still be seen.

Those who land on the island should visit the Church Cave on the east coast. A vast cavern with seats and altar of natural rock, the last service was held here in the 19thC. There are trips from Portree to view Rona.

Soay

Highland. Three miles due west of Elgol, rising to 455 ft at the summit of Beinn Bhreac, Soay (pronounced soy) is pinched into a central isthmus by the narrow cut of the harbour on the north-west coast, and by the bay of Camas nan Gall on the south-east, where the islanders live. Composed of Torridonian sandstone, it has many sea cliffs but is not very fertile.

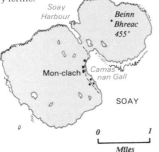

Before 1823 only one family lived here, tending stock, but, as a result of the Clearances, crofters evicted from Skye settled on Soay and by 1861 the population had risen to 129.

In 1946 the author Gavin Maxwell bought the island and started a basking shark fishery, building a slip and a small factory. Lack of demand for shark oil brought it to an end three years later; the project was revived briefly by Maxwell's harpooner Tex Geddes in 1950 although the fishing was no longer based on Soay. By 19 June 1953, all except Geddes and his family had left the island, the final evacuation being made, in a blaze of publicity, aboard the SS *Hebrides*, the crofters re-settling on Mull. A succession of people seeking the quiet life then came and went until the situation stabilised, and now there is a thriving small community, whose nine telephones are now powered by solar panels. A boat from the mainland calls monthly and hires may be arranged from Arisaig and Elgol.

Eilean Donnan

This is a tidal islet at the entrance to Loch Duich, upon which stands a beautifully reconstructed medieval fortress, among splendid and dramatic scenery. The original fortress was built in 1230 on the site of earlier defensive structures, but this was destroyed in 1719 after 45 Spanish allies of the Old Pretender surrendered to a squadron of British frigates commanded by Captain Boyle. After centuries of neglect, restoration – faithful to the original plans which had been kept in Edinburgh – began in 1912 and was completed in 1932 at a cost of £250,000. Access is gained by a stone bridge and the castle is open to visitors. To the west, in Loch Alsh, are the low-lying **Eilean Tioram** and **Glas Eilean**.

The many small islands in and around Loch Hourn are dwarfed by the grandeur of the surrounding mountains. **Eilean à Phiobair**, the Piper's Island, is one of them – perhaps his playing was not all it could be, and he was sent there to practice. **Sandaig Islands**, to the north of the Loch, shelter the bay called Camusfearna by Gavin Maxwell, who wrote *Ring of Bright Water* here in 1960. The cottage he occupied was destroyed by fire, and the ruin has been cleared. Boat trips run to here from the Kyle of Lochalsh.

There are a few islets before reaching Mallaig, ferry terminal for the Small Isles Parish and Armadale, Skye.

The reconstructed medieval fortress of Eilean Donnan

The Small Isles Parish

Highland. Canna, Rum, Eigg and Muck lie as a group to the south-west of Skye and to the west of Mallaig, and they are all inhabited. Their history is that of the surrounding isles – early conversion to Christianity, Viking raids then settlement under the suzerainty of Norway, finally becoming part of the Kingdom of Scotland in 1266. Then followed the rule of the Lords of the Isles until the end of the 15thC, then feuding by the clans vying for power, the '45 rebellion, the famines and the Clearances. Today Canna, Eigg and Muck are working islands, with small communities proving that island life is viable and valuable. Rum, owned by the Nature Conservancy Council and, in spite of its size never really habitable, is now a unique open-air laboratory.

Canna

Canna's population numbers about 20. Its name comes from the Gaelic, either *Canna* (porpoise) or *Kanin* (isle of rabbits). It extends about five miles by one mile north-west of Rum and halfway between Mallaig and Lochboisdale, South Uist. A steep-sided island, it is made up of terraced Tertiary basalt which breaks down into extremely fertile soil, on which some of the earliest crops in the West Highlands are grown. Rainfall is about 60 inches each year. At the eastern end is the harbour, with the only deep-water pier in the Small Isles Parish, sheltered by the tidal island of **Sanday** which is linked to Canna by a foot-bridge.

At the eastern tip of Canna is Compass Hill (458 ft), so called due to the high metal content of the rock and the effect this has on a ship's compass. A mile to the west is Carn a Ghaill, the island's summit, 690-ft high, and three miles south-west is the isolated basalt rock of **Humla**.

The island of Sanday is crofted; and Canna itself is run as a single farm. John Lorne Campbell bought the island in 1938 from the widow of Robert Thorn, a Glasgow ship owner. Thorn had purchased the island from Donald MacNeil in 1881, after 60 years of drastic clearances during which the population fell to 48. Thorn was a benevolent and responsible man and Canna remained in good hands when John Lorne Campbell became the new owner. He is well known for his work, with Compton Mackenzie, in founding the Sea League (*see* Barra), and, together with his American wife, he has done much to preserve and further

Gaelic literature and culture, as well as making a gift of the island to the National Trust for Scotland. The people are Catholic, and Gaelic speaking; the island is viable and happy. There is a valuable stock of Highland cattle and Cheviot sheep, and early potatoes are grown on the farm.

Evidence of Viking occupation can be seen at Rubha Langanes on the north coast, where one of the finest examples of a ship burial was uncovered. The original township before the Clearances was A'Chill, to the north of the harbour, near the site of the 7thC St Columba's Chapel. Only a Celtic cross, a column and the faint patterns of lazybeds remain. To the east of the harbour is An Coroghan, a ruined tower on top of an isolated stack, where a Clanranald chief imprisoned his wife to frustrate the attentions of her lover, a MacLeod from Skye. On the south coast is a ruined convent at Rubha Sgorr nam Bán- naomha – 'the headland of holy women'.

There is no holiday accommodation, but those who wish to camp may do so, with permission.

Rum

Rum's population is about 40 (fewer in winter) – all, apart from the schoolmistress, employed by the Nature Conservancy Council. The name is pronounced Room, possibly from the Norse *Röm oe* – wide island. Commonly, and incorrectly, written as Rhum, this spelling was introduced by the Bulloughs, the English owners between 1888 and 1957. It is the largest island in the Parish, diamond-shaped (eight by eight-and-a-half miles), nearly 26,400 acres in extent and rising to a maximum height of 2664 ft at the summit of Askival in the south. It is situated nine miles south-west of Skye. Being able to support only a small population relative to its area has resulted in its being succinctly described as a wet desert.

It is of great interest to geologists, having certain formations that are quite unique. The northern and least mountainous part is Torridonian sandstone sloping gently to the sea, with a beautiful beach at Kilmory. The central high ground is Tertiary Peridotite related closely to the Cuillins of Skye, with here and there a patch of gabbro or gneiss. The western point is composed of steep-sided granite, with dramatic sheer cliffs

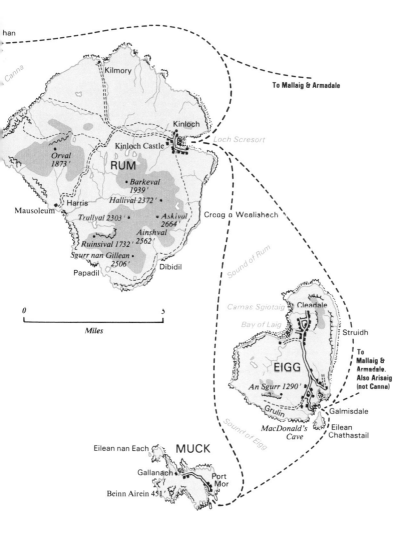

To Mallaig & Armadale

Canna

Kilmory

Kinloch

Loch Scresort

Kinloch Castle

Orval
1873'

RUM

• Barkeval
1939'

Hallival 2372'

Mausoleum   • Harris

Trullival 2303' •   • Askival
2664'

Craog a Wealishech

Ainshval
Ruinsival 1732' 2562'

Sgurr nan Gillean •
2506'   Dibidil

Papadil

Sound of Rum

0   5

Miles

Camas Sgiotaig   Cleadale

Bay of Laig   Struidh

To
Mallaig &
Armadale.
Also Arisaig
(not Canna)

EIGG

An Sgurr 1290'

Grulin   Galmisdale

MacDonald's   Eilean
Cave   Chathastail

Sound of Eigg

Eilean nan Each   MUCK

Gallanach   Port
Mor

Beinn Airein 451'

where huge blocks have tumbled pell-mell to the shore. A half a mile to the north-east of Harris is the spot which has the strongest gravitational pull in the British Isles.

The only arable land consists of a few acres at Harris in the west, Kilmory in the north and Kinloch in the east, thus little of the island can be crofted. The climate is less mild than on surrounding islands and the average yearly rainfall is 93 inches, although this varies, being as low as 56 inches at Harris and as high as 122 inches in the mountains. The topography of Rum results in prolonged periods of cloud cover

when surrounding areas may be clear, and gusty winds.

In 1346 Rum was owned by John of Islay, passing to McKenabrey of Coll in 1549, then to the MacLeans of Coll in 1695. By the early 19thC it was vastly over-crowded, and the islanders were poor and unable to pay their rent. A clearance was arranged, and over 300 souls left bound for Canada and America to face a hard winter. With about 50 people remaining, MacLean rented the land for grazing and 8000 sheep were brought in. Crofters came to the island from Skye and, by 1831, the population had

Kinloch Castle, Rum

risen to 134. The sheep proved unprofitable, and the island was sold in 1845 to the Marquis of Salisbury who stocked the streams with trout and the hills with deer. After being sold and resold, and with another attempt at sheep farming proving unsuccessful, Rum was finally bought in 1888 by the remarkable John Bullough of Oswaldtwistle, who had made his fortune designing milling machinery. It became his holiday retreat and self- contained sporting estate, with deer partly replacing the sheep.

John Bullough's son, Sir George, became the owner in 1891, and spared no expense in building Kinloch Castle, an extravagant monument to the Edwardian opulence which ended with the outbreak of war. Turtles and alligators were kept in heated tanks, a pure white Arab stallion was imported to improve the stock of the native Rum ponies (said to descend from Spanish ponies which swam ashore from a wrecked Armada galleon, but it is more likely they came from Eriskay), and two exotic Albion cars were used to transport guests. Muscatel grapes, figs, peaches and nectarines were grown under glass, and dances were held to the music of an electric organ in the sumptuous ballroom.

The island population stabilised at about 90 people until the outbreak of the war, and all regarded the Bullough family as kindly and courteous people, although the press labelled Rum 'The Forbidden Island' – a strange response to an estate kept no more private than those on the mainland. In 1957 the island was purchased from Sir George's widow, Monica Lady Bullough, by the Nature Conservancy Council to be used as a natural outdoor laboratory. Kinloch Castle has been preserved, and part is now run as a hotel.

Red deer, wild goats, domestic Highland cattle and ponies are maintained and studied. Sheltered glens are being replanted with native trees and shrubs, and open heathland is managed in order to preserve natural flora and fauna. Geology, ecology and conservation can all be studied in a unique environment, with little disturbance.

The main area of occupation is at Kinloch, where there is a shop and post office. There is no pier, and all cargo and passengers have to be trans-shipped to the jetty. Tarmac roads are also non-existent but a good track leads due west to the centre of the island, where it forks – north to Kilmory with its fine beach and cemetery with a gravestone bearing the names of six children of the Matheson family, five of whom died in the space of a week, and south to Harris and the Bullough mausoleum, built in the style of a Greek temple and not a little incongruous. A rugged track leads south from Kinloch to the east of Hallival and Askival to Dibidil and Papadil, passing near Creag-a-Wealishech – the Welshman's cliff, in memory of a gang of Welsh slate quarriers who widened a precipitous path.

The sea cliffs attract kittiwake, puffin, guillemot and razorbill and the mountain tops Manx shearwater (over 130,000 pairs). In all, over 150 species of birds have been recorded, and the sea eagle has been reintroduced using chicks taken from nests on the Norwegian coast.

Plant life is prolific and varied, little disturbed on the cliffs and mountain summits since the last ice age. There are many alpines, including the rare arctic sandwort and penny-cress; roseroot, thrift, sea campion and Scots lovage on the cliffs; bog asphodel, heath spotted-orchid, sundew, butterwort and black bog-rush on the moors.

Day visitors are welcome. Those who wish to stay longer must make *prior* arrangements with the NCC Warden at White House, Kinloch. NCC accommodation is limited and priority is given to those

Red deer stags feeding on seaweed at Kilmory, Rum. *R V Collier*

engaged in research work. Climbers require a permit and must be in organised parties. There is also accommodation at the hotel.

About nine miles west of Rum lie **Oighsgeir** and **Garbh Sgeir** (the maiden rock), hexagonal basalt columns with an area of about 10 acres, rising 33 ft above sea level. The channel between the two outcrops has often provided welcome shelter for small boats caught by storms, the spray passing overhead as the craft lie in calm water. During the 19thC, Canna cattle were grazed on the islets' lush grass. The lighthouse was built in 1902 by D A Stevenson, and is destined soon to become automatic. Meanwhile the three lighthouse keepers grow vegetables and flowers in what must be the country's most remote walled gardens, as well as fishing lobsters and relaxing on the miniature golf course they have built .

Eigg

Pronounced egg, the name is probably derived from the Gaelic *eige* (a hollow) and was once know as *Eilean Nimban-More* (island of the big women). It has an area of over 5000 acres and is dominated by An Sgurr at the southern end, the largest mass of columnar pitchstone lava in Britain, rising a sheer 290 ft above the 1000 ft contour, best seen from the south, with a view from the top that is superb. A large colony of Manx shearwater has established itself on An Sgurr, burrowing into the soil.

The northern plateau and southern moor are basalt and have weathered into excellent soil. Cliffs around the northern point are sandstone, eroded into fantastic shapes at Camas Sgiotaig, where the beach is composed of grains of quartz, white with black flecks, which creak underfoot – Eigg's famous singing sands (but only when they are dry). To the north of the pretty Bay of Laig there are limestone blocks and nodules, some trapped in rock cages and rattled by the waves. The crofting township of Cleadale lies behind the bay.

Eigg's main village is Galmisdale, on the south-east corner, its small pier partially sheltered by the columnar basalt **Eilean Chathastail** (castle island) with its lighthouse. The harbour is not deep but can be used by launches.

Half a mile south-west of the pier is MacDonalds Cave or Uamh Fhraing (St Francis Cave), where, in the winter of 1577 (after an exchange of minor atrocities) the MacLeods of Skye suffocated 395 MacDonalds by burning brushwood at the narrow entrance. The MacDonalds were undiscovered until one of their scouts was spotted by the MacLeods who then traced his footprints in the snow leading to the cave. The feuding continued at Trumpan in Skye. A little further to the west is Cathedral Cave, used by Roman Catholics during the time of their persecution; a stone wall in the cave may have served as an altar. In the 7thC, a monastery was founded by St Donnan, who, with his brothers, was killed by the islanders. The building was later destroyed by Norsemen, and the ruins of the 14thC Kildonnan Church stand on the site of this earlier building.

MacDonald of Clanranald was given the island by Robert the Bruce in 1309. The Clan supported the Prince during the unsuccessful '45 rebellion. Captain John Ferguson of the King's ship, *Furnace*, later visited Eigg to arrest John MacDonald, who surrendered to avoid bloodshed. Ferguson gave an undertaking that, if the MacDonalds gave up their weapons, there would be no reprisals. After agreeing to this, those who were suspected of supporting the rebellion were taken, the island was sacked and the young men transported.

The MacDonalds sold Eigg in 1827 for £15,000 to Dr Hugh MacPherson, and several clearances took place. Upon his death the island passed to his children and became relatively prosperous during the 1870s, the population at this time being over 300. In the 1890s it was bought by Robert Thompson, and again the island prospered, but he died a sick and lonely man. He was buried beneath a marble slab at the summit of Eilean Cathastail on Christmas Day, 1913.

In the 1920s the island was purchased by the Runciman family, who developed the land, ploughed back profits, and made a self-sufficient and mechanised 2000-acre farm. In 1966 it was sold to Robert Evans, a Welsh Border farmer, who in turn sold it in 1971 to a Christian charity, which succeeded in alienating and demoralising the whole population with grandiose schemes that took no account of the island's needs.

In 1975 it was purchased by the present owner and is now actively promoted as a holiday island. There is guest-house, caravan and cottage accommodation available, but demand usually exceeds supply. Its resident population numbers about 60.

Muck

The name comes from the Gaelic, *eilean a muic* (isle of the sow), and was referred to by Buchanan in 1582 as *insula porcorum* (pigs' island). With an area of 1586 acres, rising to a maximum height of 451 ft at the summit of Beinn Airein, it lies about two-and-a-half miles south-west of Eigg and eight miles north of Ardnamurchan. A fertile island of Tertiary basalt, which receives beneficial dressings of wind-blown shell sand, it is a pretty and peaceful place with pleasant beaches, even if somewhat exposed to the weather. At the south-east corner is Port Mor, a small harbour with a difficult rocky entrance. Off the north-west tip, **Eilean nan Each** (horse island), where ponies were kept, and **Eilean Aird nan Uan** (the lambs' lofty isle) can be reached at low tide.

Muck is run as a single unit by Lawrence MacEwan, a caring and tenacious laird who keeps cattle, sheep and a small dairy herd, and grows potatoes, oats and root crops – quite an achevement on what is truly an oceanic island. The laird's house is at Gallanach.

In 1828, 150 kelp collectors were cleared and in 1854 Captain Thomas Swinburne, RN, the new owner, began a fishing industry, renting the land out for sheep. By 1861 the population was 58; today it is about 25.

There are a few acres of woodland, and in spring and early summer the fields are coloured by cornflower, harebell, marigold and iris. Above Port Mor there is a ruined chapel by the graveyard, and at the entrance to the harbour are the few remains of a defensive structure, the Castle of the White Fort. There is a limited amount of holiday accommodation at the guest house or holiday cottage. Tents may be used.

The Small Isles Parish is served by Caledonian MacBrayne's ferry *Lochmor* from Mallaig via Armadale on Skye, which does a round trip three times each week. There are also boats from Mallaig and Arisaig during the summer serving Eigg and Rum and a ferry from Glenuig and Lochailort, to Eigg, also during the summer only.

Maillaig to Loch Linnhe

At the entrance to Loch nan Ceall (loch of the hermit's cell), there are many islands and rocks, the largest being the tidal **Eilean Ighe** and **Luinga Mhór**. At the head of the loch is Arisaig, beautifully situated and an embarkation point for boat trips to Rum, Eigg and Muck.

On **Eilean a' Ghaill**, to the south-east of Rubh' Arisaig, are the remains of a fort; there are others on Rubh' Aird Ghamhsgail, on the northern shore of Loch nan Uamh, and on **Eilean nan Gobhar** (goat island) at the entrance to Loch Ailort. Loch nan Uamh (loch of the caves) was the scene of the end of the '45 Rising, where Prince Charlie, after his adventures in the Outer Hebrides and on Skye with Flora MacDonald, finally left Scotland for the last time aboard the *Heureux*. A cairn has been erected to mark this historic event. On the southern shore of the Sound of Arisaig is the tidal **Samalaman Island** with a fine sandy beach and picnic area.

Eilean Shona (island of the ford) splits the entrance to Loch Moidart, and is extensively forested on the eastern side; composed mainly of rugged igneous rock, it rises to a height of 870 ft. The *New Statistical Account of Scotland* of 1845 says that it was 'the only island worth noticing' in Ardnamurchan and that 'the dwelling

Opposite: An Sgurr, Eigg. *Holiday Which?*

house and surrounding scenery of the residence of a respectable family are very beautiful.' It has a population of about 10, and the whole was offered for sale in 1981 for £1½ million. The private estate has a deer herd, oyster fisheries, plantations and wild cat estimated to be 4 ft long. The dramatist James Barrie wrote *Mary Rose* whilst staying here.

To the south is the wooded **Riska Island**, and Castle Tioram (or *Tirrin*, the dry castle) standing on a rocky tidal islet off Cùl Doirlinn in the beautiful Loch Moidart. Built in the 13thC, it was the seat of the Mac-Donalds of Clanranald, and around 1600 some domestic buildings were added to the original massive curtain walls. This area was the centre of both Jacobite risings in 1715 and 1745. The castle was partly destroyed, at the orders of Clanranald, after

the failure of the '45, although parts remained habitable. The unfortunate Lady Grange spent some time here *en route* to her exile on St Kilda.

In Loch Sunart are the islands of **Risga, Carna** and **Oronsay**; their position in the entrance to the loch causes the tide to flow swiftly around them. Oronsay, low-lying, barren and rocky, deeply indented with sea lochs, was once inhabited, as was Carna, recorded in 1845 as being a more fertile island. Seals breed around **Eilean nan Eildean** to the west, and can also be seen in Glenmore Bay, sheltered by the tidal **Eilean Mór**.

The island of Risga has cup-marked rocks which may have been part of some kind of moon and sun calendar. It is the breeding ground of oystercatcher, merganser, eider duck and tern.

Mull

Strathclyde. The name Mull means mass of hill, an apt description for this volcanic island, the third largest in the Hebrides. With an area of nearly 225,000 acres, it lies to the west of Oban, its east coast roughly parallel to the Morven shore. In the south, the Ross of Mull extends as a long peninsula, with the island of Iona off the tip, and the west is deeply indented with sea lochs leaving only a narrow neck of land between Loch na Keal and Salen.

The highest point, at the summit of Ben More, is 3170 ft and there are several other peaks well over 2000 ft. Most characteristic of the landscape are the terraced hills known as trap – Tertiary basalt plateau lavas, the volcanic outpourings of 40-50 million years ago, now much eroded. These stepped hillsides are best seen around Loch Scridain. The mountain of Ben More is the highest Tertiary basalt in Britain – the trap layers beneath the summit end in dramatic sea cliffs at Ardmeanach. Later eruptions, centred on Beinn Chàsgidle and Loch Bà, formed circular granitic dykes some five miles in diameter and 300-ft thick – the collapsed cores of the vents.

Northern Mull is plateau basalt, flat wet moorland rising to the trap layers, never higher than 1500 ft. 'S Airde Beinn is a volcanic plug. On the headland south of Treshnish Point there is a pre-glacial raised beach, 125-ft high and fertile, and in the south-east, Loch Spelve and Loch Buie are the end of the Great Glen fault. Glen More has many glacial features, including a terminal moraine above Graig Cottage.

Westward along the Ross of Mull the

To Lochbois

To Coll and

Port na Caila

Calgary

Craickaig

Treshnish Isles

Gometra

Little Co

Staffa

M

Kintra

Iona

Fionnphort

Erraid

Fidden

Torran Rocks

trap country gives way first to crystalline gneiss and then to a boss of pink granite, four miles square. Beneath the basalt lavas is a thin layer of chalk, exposed at Carsaig where lime-laden water washes over lias on a south-facing coast, giving extremely favourable growing conditions. Here, as in the chalk streams of southern England, watercress grows.

Columnar balsalt, which perhaps reaches its apogee on Staffa, is also to be found on Ulva and Gometra, near Tavool on Ardmeanach and near Bunessan and at Carsaig. The east coast, sheltered from the erosive forces of the prevailing weather, consists of raised beaches above shallow bays.

Mull's climate is mild Atlantic, with very high rainfall in the mountains, making the growing season long. Wind is funnelled to the island's centre by the sea lochs.

The largest landowner and main source of employment is the Forestry Commission who have vast plantations of Sitka spruce and larch in the north-east, at Ardmeanach and on the Ross of Mull. There are a few large farms, a little crofting centred on the Ross and large areas of deer forest. Since the introduction of large-scale sheep farming in the 19thC and the consequent despoilation of cultivated land, Mull's considerable agricultural potential has never been fully realised – a fact reflected by the tiny population of 1600. The lobster fishing industry thrives (in the 1920s a 12-pounder was

Ben More towering over Loch Scridain, Mull

taken in Calgary Bay) and there are, of course, tourists coming in ever-increasing numbers.

The first inhabitants of Mull left stones, circles and cairns scattered over the island. Crannogs (lake dwellings) were built on stilts in Lochs Bà, Assapol, Frisa, Sguabain, Poit na h-I and na Keal. The Irish Celts came in the 2ndC, a turbulent period when many forts and duns were built; there are fine examples at Dùn Aisgain to the north of Loch Tuath; Dùn Urgadul (vitrified) one mile north of Tobermory; Dùn nan Gall (fort of the stranger) on Loch Tuath; and An Sean Dùn (the bewitched fort), south-west of Glengorm – the last two being brochs.

Christianity came to Iona with the arrival of St Columba in AD 563. The Norsemen raided then settled, and Mull came under Norwegian suzerainty until 1266 when, along with the other islands, it was controlled by Scotland under the Lordship of the Isles. Following this period, the MacLeans became the dominant clan on Mull until the clan system was forcibly broken after the '45 rebellion.

During the 18thC the population increased rapidly, peaking at 10,600 in 1821. There was enormous pressure on the land, although the kelp industry alone sustained many people until it collapsed in 1852. Emigration began even before the lairds and newcomers began clearing the land for sheep, and many evictions were made by owners with little regard for the hardships caused. An exception was the Duke of Argyll, who tried to find employment for his tenants. However, by 1881 the population had been halved, and the Crofters' Act of 1886 did little to help matters,

many of the remaining crofts being amalgamated into larger farming units. When the grazings were ruined, the Victorians turned to the sporting potential of the island, stocking it with red deer, which are now to be seen around Torosay, Laggan and Ben More.

Craignure to Tobermory

The main ferry terminal on Mull is at Craignure, where the new pier was built in 1964 to take the large vehicle ferry from Oban. To the north, beyond Scalastle Bay, is the terminal for the much smaller Lochaline – Fishnish vehicle ferry. The airstrip in Glenforsa was built in 54 days in 1966 by the 38th Engineer Regiment as an exercise.

At Pennygown only the walls remain of a medieval chapel; inside is the shaft of a Celtic cross, probably brought from Iona, showing the Virgin and Child. It is said that there were once benevolent fairies here who would complete any task that was left on their mound – spinning, weaving or the like – until someone left a short piece of wood, asking them to make a ship's mast. After that, no more favours were done.

Salen village sits in a wide bay at the mid-point of the Sound of Mull, and is a convenient touring centre for the island. At the north of the bay are the ruins of Aros Castle, built in the 14thC by the Lord of the Isles, and last occupied in 1608, beneath which treasure from the Tobermory galleon is said to lie buried.

There are several small islands in the Sound of Mull. At the southern entrance close to the mainland, beyond the lighthouse on **Glas Eileanan**, is **Eilean Rubha an Ridire**. In 1973 divers discovered the wreck of the 17thC Royal Navy frigate *Dartmouth* off the north-west shore: she was torn from

The fine harbour of Tobermory, Mull

her moorings in the Sound during a storm and was wrecked on 19 October 1690. Off Salen is **Eileanan Glasa** where, on 25 January 1935, the cargo ship *Rondo* was wrecked, totally demolishing the original lighthouse.

At the northern end of the Sound is the beautiful harbour of Tobermory (*Tobar Mhoire*, Mary's well), full of visiting yachts in the summer and sheltered by **Calve Island** (used as a summer residence) and the steep hills behind. This colourful town is one of the smallest to have had burgh status (from 1875 to 1975), with a population of about 700. The port was developed by the British Fisheries Society in 1788, who built the fine stone houses in the main street, now brightly painted and giving the town a Continental atmosphere. The courthouse, built in 1862, serves as the police station and council offices. There are hotels, a museum, boarding houses, a tourist information office, a youth hostel, shops, bank, library, petrol stations, good junior and senior schools, and a fine public park – the Aros House Policies – given to the town by the Forestry Commission in 1969. There is also a nine-hole golf course.

Buried in the mud at the bottom of the bay lie the remains of a galleon from the routed Spanish Armada, which went down while undergoing repairs in 1588. Long thought to be the *Almirante de Florencia* carrying 30 million ducats, it attracted many salvage attempts, none of which retrieved anything of great monetary value but destroyed a historical site potentially as valuable as that of the *Mary Rose* in the Solent. Recent research by Alison McLeay, documented in her excellent book 'The

Tobermory Treasure', has shown beyond reasonable doubt that it was the *San Juan de Sicilia*, a Ragusan ship from what is now Dubrovnik, which foundered here after a fierce fire on board. Stories that it was sabotaged by Donald MacLean, imprisoned on board, are without foundation. To the north is Bloody Bay, scene of a battle between John, last Lord of the Isles, and his son Angus.

A minor road west from Tobermory passes Dùn Urgadul, a vitrified fort, before ending at the private Glengorm Castle (built 1860), well situated near the windswept Mishnish headland. Glengorm means blue glen, a name suggested to the unwitting owner and which referred to the blue smoke of the burning crofts when the area was cleared. The main road to Dervaig passes the three Mishnish lochs, set in wild open moorland and well stocked with trout.

Dervaig to Ardmeanach

The pretty village of Dervaig (the little grove), sitting at the head of Loch a' Chumhainn, was built by the MacLeans of Coll in 1799. By the road is the Kilmore Parish Church which has a pencil steeple, more commonly seen in Ireland, and an attractive interior. The Mull Little Theatre was founded in the village, and to the south is The Old Byre, with its unusual tableaux of crofting life. The road south-east to Aros passes Loch Frisa (a trout fishery) and, just before its summit Druimtigh-macgillechattan, Mull's longest place-name and site of an ancient market which was held at the ridge of the house of the Cattenach fellow.

At the mouth of Loch a' Chumhainn is Croig, a little rocky inlet where cattle from the outer isles were once landed on their way to the mainland. At Calgary there is a

The deserted village of Crackaig, Mull

fine sweep of pale sand backed by machair and, on the northern side, by the old pier, is a prominent basalt dyke which may have given the bay its name – *Calagharaidh*, the haven by the wall. The city of Calgary in Canada was *not* so named by emigrants from Mull, contrary to popular belief.

The road south passes the gaunt ruin of Reudle schoolhouse, standing alone on the moor. About a mile south-west along the valley are the substantial remains of Crackaig and Clac Gugairidh, the hollow of the dark grazings, overlooking the Treshnish Isles; 200 people lived in these two villages until the end of the last century. The ash tree where a villager hanged himself still grows in the walled garden by the burn, and below in the cliffs is the Still Cave, where illicit whisky was made.

At Kilninian there is a small area of fine natural woodland and beyond this, near Ulva Ferry, a waterfall. The view across Loch Tuath to the trap hills of **Ulva** and **Gometra** is excellent. These islands, with **Little Colonsay**, were the scene of an almost total clearance of 600 inhabitants by F. W. Clark between 1846 and 1851. Ulva (wolf island) was held by the MacQuarries for 800 years until the 18thC; there was once a piping college founded by a MacArthur, a pupil of the famed McCrimmons of Skye, and Ulva House stands in fine woodland on the site of an earlier house once visited by Sir Walter Scott. Ulva and Gometra are joined by a bridge. The latter was once the home of Himalayan explorer Hugh Ruttledge. Little Colonsay was once farmed by a single family, living in a surprisingly large Victorian farmhouse, until forced to leave by a plague of rats. The islands now support sheep and some cattle, and are being steadily improved after the depredations which followed the Clearances. They are private, and permission to visit is at the discretion of the owners.

The island of **Eorsa**, in Loch na Keal (the loch of the cliffs), once belonged to the Priory of Iona – it is grazed by a few sheep and has a ruined bothy at the eastern end. The southern shore of the loch is dramatic, the slopes of Ben More (which is most easily climbed from Dhiseig) falling steeply to the water. At Gribun there are huge boulders which have fallen from the cliffs – one of these, now lying by a stone wall, flattened a small cottage in which two newlyweds lay sleeping.

Off the Gribun shore is **Inch Kenneth** – flat, fertile and farmed it was once the granary of Iona. There is a ruined chapel but no remains of the accompanying monastery. Sir Alan MacLean's grave in the burial ground is covered by an intricately carved slab showing the Chief in armour with his dog at his feet. The island is private.

One mile south of Balmeanach is Mackinnon's Cave, about 100-ft high and 600-ft deep, with stalactites in the deepest part. It can only be entered at low tide, and a torch is helpful. At Rubha na h-Uamha, which is the most westerly point of the boulder-strewn cliffs of the wild Ardmeanach peninsula, is MacCulloch's Tree, a fossil 40-ft high, engulfed by lava 50 million years ago. It was first described by Dr MacCulloch in 1819, and can be reached either from Balmeanach or Tiroran on Loch Scridain, where there is a National Trust for Scotland office. The walk along the shore is difficult but fascinating; try to arrive at half tide on the ebb.

The south-west end of Ardmeanach, known as the Burgh, was given to the National Trust for Scotland in 1932 by A. Campbell Blair of Dolgellau. It is a natural reserve for red deer, wild goat, otter, golden eagle, hen harrier, peregrine, sparrowhawk, buzzard and numerous smaller birds.

To the east of Tiroran the road skirts Loch Scridain to join the main Craignure-

Duart Castle

Fionnphort road. To the south of Craignure is Torosay Castle, designed in the Scottish baronial style by David Bryce and built in 1856. The name means a hill covered with shrubs, and beautiful gardens, designed by Sir Robert Lorimer around formal Italianate terraces in 1899 slope down to the shore, and are open to the public.

Duart Castle and The Ross

Duart Castle stands on a dark headland, the imposing ancestral home of the MacLeans since about 1250. Overrun and put to fire by the Duke of Argyll in 1691, it was only returned to MacLean hands in 1912, and is now the residence of the 27th Chief and his wife, having been lovingly restored from ruins. It is open to the public who can explore the keep, battlements, and cells, examine MacLean relics, and see a scouting exhibition. On the coast to the south, at the entrance to Loch Don, is Grass Point, terminal for the old Oban – Kerrera – Mull ferry, and start of the pilgrim's path to Iona. Further south, at the entrance to Loch Spelve, is Port nam Marbh, the port of the dead where corpses were landed from the mainland for burial on Iona. A minor road west passes along the northern shores of Lochs Spelve and Uisg, through attractive scenery and mixed woodlands with masses of rhododendrons to Lochbuie. Moy Castle, built in the 15thC by the MacLeans of Lochbuie, is a sturdy tower with a spring in the natural rock floor. Unfortunately there is no public access. Two miles to the east of the mouth of Loch Buie is the interestingly-named **Frank Lockwood's Island** – he was Solicitor General in Lord Rosebery's administration 1894-5 and brother-in-law of the 21st MacLean of Lochbuie.

The main road passes through the bare, glaciated Glen More, above the Lussa River. The Glen once separated the kingdoms of the Picts and the Scots (Dalriada). A cairn at Pedlars Pool marks the spot where a pedlar,

who took care of two households with smallpox, died of the disease himself, and another cairn at Pennyghael commemorates the Beatons, hereditary doctors to the Lords of the Isles. A minor road south across the moor finishes at the fertile valley and farm at Carsaig. Along the shore to the west is the Nun's Cave, which contains early Christian carvings. Sandstone was quarried nearby until 1873, and was used in Iona Cathedral. Two miles beyond the cave at Malcolm's Point, beneath 700 ft cliffs, are the dark red basaltic Carsaig Arches.

The coast of the Ross is broken with many small bays and some fine beaches, such as that at Uisken; Bunessan is the touring centre for this area. Inland is windswept, undulating moorland. The road finishes at Fionnphort, where the ferry leaves for Iona. Half a mile to the north granite was quarried until the late 19thC; stone from here was used to build Holborn Viaduct, Blackfriars Bridge and the Albert Memorial in London, and the Skerryvore and Dubh Artach lighthouses. Further north is the pretty harbour of Kintra. To the south, beyond the fine beach at Fidden, is the tidal island of **Erraid**, featured in Robert Louis Stevenson's book *Kidnapped*, which he is said to have written in one of the houses behind the row of granite cottages used as the shore station for the Dubh Artach and Skerryvore lighthouses (*see* Tiree) until 1967. In the book, David Balfour thought himself stranded on Erraid after the brig *Covenant* was wrecked on the seaward side – not realising that he could cross the sand at low tide. At the summit of Crioc Mor is the iron observatory once used to signal to the lighthouses. The island is now occupied by members of the Findhorn Community.

The Dubh Artach lighthouse marks the end of a reef running south from Mull, which manifests itself as the Torran Rocks (*torunn* means a loud murmuring noise).

The tidal island of Erraid, Mull

The lighthouse, which became operational in 1872, was designed by Thomas and David Stevenson, R.L.S.'s father and uncle respectively. From base of the tower to the base of the lantern measures 106 ft, and it is built on a rock 35 ft above mean high water.

Although Mull's proximity to the mainland is making it increasingly popular with tourists, it is still easy to find vast open spaces with no one else around.

Caledonian MacBrayne operate the vehicle ferry *Isle of Mull* between Oban and Craignure, the voyage taking 40 minutes; and they also operate a smaller vehicle ferry, the *Isle of Cumbrae*, between Lochaline and Fishnish, with a journey time of 15 minutes. The vehicle ferry *Lord of the Isles* from Oban to Coll and Tiree calls at Tobermory for passengers only, and the *Coll* operates between Kilchoan and Tobermory for passengers only. Loganair fly to Glenforsa from Glasgow. Excursions are run from Oban to Mull and Iona. There is a bus service on Mull, and the Tourist Information Centre is in Tobermory.

Treshnish Isles

These are a string of volcanic islands lying on a south-west/north-east axis, about three-and-a-half miles west of Gometra, off Mull and designated since 1974 as a Site of Special Scientific Interest. At the southern end, and separated from the rest of the group, is **Bac Mór**, the Dutchman's Cap, its old lava cone encircled by a lava rim – a distinctive landmark. The central and largest island is **Lunga**, rising to 338 ft at the summit of Cruachan, below which are the remains of some black houses, last occupied in 1857 as summer sheilings: permanent occupation ended in 1824 when Donald Campbell and his family finally left. On the west coast are

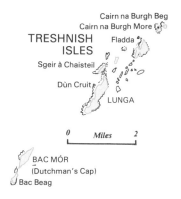

the sea-bird cliffs and pinnacle of Dùn Cruit. 25 species of sea birds breed on the islands, and barnacle geese winter here. Sheep still graze the larger islands, and grey seals breed among the rocks by the shore.

To the north-east of Lunga, across a profusion of rocks and skerries, is **Fladda**, once occupied each summer by a lobster fisherman. On the island of **Cairn na Burgh More** are the remains of a fort believed to have belonged to the Chief of Clan MacDougall, Lord of Lorn, on the site of an older Norse building. It once marked the division between the Nordreys (Northern isles) and the Sudreys (southern isles), and was given up to the Lord of the Isles in 1354. Religious books and records from Iona were said to have been hidden here at the time of the Reformation; when Cromwell took the fort in 1650, the books were lost although recent research has called the whole story into question. In 1715 it was held by the MacLeans of Duart. There are the remains of a small chapel, and the Well of the Half Gallon.

The Treshnish Isles

On **Cairn na Burgh Beg** are the ruins of a smaller fort occupied during the 1715 Jacobite rising.

Cruises around the Treshnish Isles are arranged from Ulva Ferry and Fionnphort on Mull. The islands look quite spectacular when viewed from the ruined village of Crackaig on Mull. Bought by the late Colonel Rankine, explorer and naturalist, in 1938, permission to land must be obtained from the family at Treshnish House on Mull.

Staffa

This is a tiny island that is known worldwide. It covers 71 acres, rising to a maximum height of 135 ft, and the name derives from the Norse *stafr-ey* (pillar or

post island), after the wooden posts the Norsemen set vertically to build their houses. Staffa resulted from the same volcanic activity which formed the Giant's Causeway in Ireland and the Ardmeanach promontory on Mull, six miles to the southeast, and consists of grey-black fine-grained Tertiary basalt surmounted by amorphous lava, the basalt lavas having cooled slowly, resulting in patterns of three breaks radiating from single points equidistant over the surface, relieving the tension evenly. The results are the spectacular hexagonal columns which gave Staffa its name.

Perhaps more famous than the island itself is Fingal's Cave, a cavern among the pillars at the southern tip, 65 ft high, 50 ft wide and 123 ft deep. Although flooded by the sea, it is possible to walk inside along natural causeways. It may be named after Fionn MacCaul, a legendary Celtic giant who is supposed to have built the Giant's Causeway, and in Gaelic it is known as *An Uamh Binn*, the melodious cave – the sea makes strange noises among the pillars. A musical tribute was made to the cavern by Felix Mendelssohn in his *Hebrides Overture* after he visited Staffa in 1829. From inside the cave, the view south is of Iona, and to the west of the cave is the Great Face or Colonnade, an expanse of columns about 55 ft tall, below which is Boat Cave. The cliff near Fingal's Cave was marked by a mine which exploded in May 1945.

On the west side of Staffa is Port an Fhasgaidh (shelter bay), a strange name considering its exposure to the prevailing weather. To the south is MacKinnon's Cave, nearly as grand as Fingal's and connected to Cormorant's Cave by a narrow tunnel. It is traditionally thought to be named after Abbot MacKinnon (died c. 1500), Abbot of Iona.

Staffa. Fingal's Cave is on the far right. *Scottish Tourist Board*

Off the south-east shore is **Am Buachaille** (the herdsman), a columnar rock separated from Staffa by 15 ft of water. Opposite the southern end is a peculiar formation known as the Wishing Chair. A little to the north is the usual landing place, Clamshell Cave – its strikingly curved columns give it its name. Little of all this can be seen from the island's grassy summit; a boat affords the best view.

Staffa was, of course, known to the local people, and to the Norsemen, long before it was discovered by the President of the Royal Society, Sir Joseph Banks, on 13 August 1772, while on his way to Iceland. After him followed a stream of visitors, and soon paddle-steamers were bringing hundreds of tourists. Among those who made the trip were: Sir Walter Scott in 1810, John Keats in 1818, Mendelssohn in 1829, J. M. W. Turner in 1830, William Wordsworth, Queen Victoria and Prince Albert in 1833, Jules Verne in 1859 (he featured Staffa in his book, *The Green Ray* in 1885), Dr David Livingstone in 1864 and Robert Louis Stevenson in 1870. In August 1884 two tourists off the paddle steamer *Chevalier* were drowned in Fingal's Cave. When Banks first came, the island had only one inhabitant, a herdsman living in a rough hut; by 1784 there were 16 people and livestock and in 1788 it was recorded that barley, oats, flax and potatoes were grown near the island's centre. Permanent habitation ceased at the end of the 18thC, although a herdsman continued to come for the summer grazing. In 1800 there were three red deer. Now there is a resident herd of black cattle.

On the shore of Lake Zurich in Switzerland is the town of Stäfa, founded by one of Iona's monks who took memories of this extraordinary little island with him on his journey. Boat trips to the island are run from Iona. Staffa is owned by the National Trust for Scotland.

Iona

Strathclyde. An island of great Christian importance, Iona is three-and-a-half miles by one-and-a-half miles, lying three-quarters of a mile off the Ross of Mull. It consists of low-lying Torridonian sandstone, with Archaean gneiss on the western side – it is not related geologically to Mull. The highest point is Dùn-I (pronounced doon-ee) in the north, rising to 332 ft; there is another small hill in the south, and the valley between

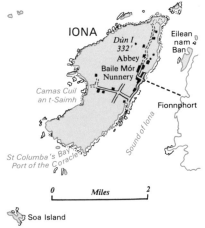

The Cathedral Church of St Mary, Iona

these two points is farmed, more so to the east. In the west, Camas Cuil an t-Saimh (the bay at the back of the ocean) is backed by machair, and Iona marble was quarried near Cùl Bhuirg. The southern coast comprises cliffs and bays; the north has sandy beaches and machair. The main area of settlement and ferry terminal is Baile Mór facing Fionnphort, where there are hotels, shops, restaurants and a post office.

The island was used by Druids before the birth of Christ, and was known in Gaelic as *Innis nan Druinich* (isle of the Druidic hermits). It was also called *Ioua* and, later, *I-Chaluim-cille* (island of St Columba); during the 1500s it was once again known as Ioua, finally to become Iona. St Columba landed here from Ireland in AD 563 to found a monastery, a centre from which the mainland Picts could be converted. St Columba lived on the island for 34 years until his death in AD 597. Under his influence, Iona became the Christian centre of Europe (the *Book of Kells*, now in Dublin was begun here), but was later destroyed by the Norsemen who raided in the years 795, 801, 806 (killing 68 monks at Martyrs Bay near the jetty), 825 and 986 (when the abbot and 15 monks were massacred at the White Strand).

In 1074 the monastery was rebuilt by St Margaret, Queen of Scotland, for the Roman Catholic order of St Augustine, and it was again rebuilt in 1203 by Reginald of Islay, King of the Isles and Somerled's son, for the Benedictine order. He also built the convent; much of this fine pink granite building remains, covered with grass and wild flowers. In 1430 the Bishopric of the Isles was created, with a seat in Iona, and in 1500 Iona achieved cathedral status. During the Reformation, all the ecclesiastical buildings were dismantled and nearly all the island's 350 crosses were destroyed. Taken by MacLean of Duart in 1574, the island was re-taken by Argyll in 1688. The ruins of the abbey

church were gifted to the Church of Scotland, in 1899, and were restored by 1910.

The monastic buildings were restored by the Iona Community between 1938 and 1965. Recently the island, excluding the cathedral area, was bought on behalf of the Scottish nation from the Duke of Argyll by the Fraser Foundation, and recently gifted to the National Trust for Scotland.

The Cathedral Church of St Mary is a simple cruciform building with a short tower, built in scale with its surroundings. The 10thC crosses of St Martin and St John (a replica), both standing near the west door, are beautiful, but no equal to the Kildalton High Cross on Islay; behind them is the tiny St Columba's shrine. The infirmary museum houses a collection of curved slabs, and along the marble causeway known as the Street of the Dead is St Oran's Chapel. It was recorded in 1549 that 60 kings – 48 Scottish, 4 Irish and 8 Norwegian – were buried in the graveyard, Reilig Odhrain, including Duncan who was murdered by Macbeth. The tombs have long since vanished.

The Iona Community was founded in the 1930s by George MacLeod (now the Very Rev. Lord MacLeod of Fuinary), and was known as the Rome Express by the Scottish Presbyterians. Their work in rebuilding Iona was to make possible an experiment in full Christian living. Today the Community numbers 150, with 600 associate members worldwide. It is especially concerned with what it calls industrial evangelism, its members working in industry, depressed city areas and new towns. The MacLeod Centre, opened in August 1988, accommodates 50 guests each week who come to share the life of the community, still finding Iona a place of retreat, regeneration and inspiration.

Each year 500,000 visitors, mainly day-trippers, come to the island. Most stray no further than the village and the cathedral

and, with such an influx to cope with, it is inevitable that this area has a touristy feel. But wander further, and peace and natural beauty can be found.

On the south coast are St Columba's Bay and the Port of the Coracle, where St Columba landed. Along here are beautifully coloured pebbles of green serpentine, and one-and-a-half miles offshore is the low-lying **Soa Island**. South of the village are two fine white shell-sand bays, backed by heather and wild flowers. From the modest summit of **Dùn-I** may be seen a panorama of the Inner Hebrides and, to the south of this hill below a hillock called Tor Abb in the Secluded Hollow, are the foundations of a hermit's cell, traditionally considered to be a spot frequented by St Columba. **Eilean nam Ban**, in the Sound of Iona, is said to be where St Columba sent all the women from Iona during his lifetime.

The island's main income is derived from visitors, but the main source of employment is crofting. On the fine west-coast farmlands, with sandy beaches backed by machair and secluded bays with semi-precious stones, Iona's other, more typically Hebridean, life goes on untouched by the thousands of visitors. The permanent population (excluding the Community) now numbers 100.

Iona is reached by the Caledonian MacBrayne passenger ferry *Morvern* from Fionnphort, Mull. There are trips from Oban during the summer by ferry *Isle of Mull* and special coach over Mull to connect with *Morvern* at Fionnphort. Cruises to Staffa are run from Iona.

Lismore

Strathclyde. Covering 10,000 acres, Lismore measures nine-and-a-half miles by one-and-three-quarter miles, and lies in Loch Linnhe to the north of Oban. Its Gaelic name is *Ieis Mor* (the great garden). It is composed of Dalradian limestone, with shallow longitudinal valleys that provide shelter for livestock, and good farming conditions on extremely fertile soil. The highest point is Barr Mór (416 ft). There is now little natural woodland although, in 1596, the island was reported to have been thickly forested with oak; however, some splendid trees have now been planted around the well cared for 19thC farmhouses. An influx of younger people into the farming community has begun to revitalise the island, which has probably never reached its full potential as rearing ground for cattle and sheep.

Until half a century ago limestone was quarried at An Sailean and shipped to the surrounding islands and mainland, and two

The Lismore ferry, Port Appin

quarrymen's cottages and some lime kilns can still be seen on the tiny **Eilean nan Caorach** off the northern tip. Many lime-carrying boats operated from Port Ramsay close by, where there is a sheltered anchorage and two attractive rows of neat cottages, now used mainly as holiday homes. The view from here along Loch Linnhe towards Ben Nevis is superb.

Lismore was the seat of the diocese of Argyll from the 13thC until 1507, the bishops receiving the title *Episcopi Lismorenses*. Incorporated into the tiny parish church are parts of the choir of the original medieval cathedral, and on the west coast, facing Bernera Island, are the ruins of the Bishop's Castle, Achadun. **Bernera Island** is also known as Berneray an Iubhar Uasail, Berneray of the Noble Yew. Dean Munro wrote in the 16thC that it was a holy place associated with St Columba, who preached under the yew, which is said to have been felled in 1850 to build a staircase in Lochnell Castle on the mainland. There are no remains of the small chapel which once existed.

In the 6thC a legendary race for posession of Lismore took place between St Moluag and St Mulhac: whoever made the first landfall would take possession. It is said that St Moluag, on seeing that his boat would not be first, cut off his finger and threw it ashore, thus securing the title. St Moluag did, however, found a monastery on Lismore between AD 561 and 564. Some 30 years ago the *buchull mor* (pastoral staff) of St Moluag was brought back to the island.

There is one main road running almost the length of the island, and most of the dwellings are sited by it, with the majority in the north; near the centre there is a post office, general store, and a junior school. Much of Lismore is owned by the Duke of Argyll, and is farmed by tenants, the present population numbering 160. There is no mains water, the houses being supplied by springs which are vulnerable should there be a long dry spell. Much of the shoreline is low sea cliffs, with some pleasant shingle beaches, and on the east side, and off the northern tip, there are some small islands, rocks and skerries. Between Eilean Musdile, off Lismore's south west tip, and Duart Point can be seen Lady's Rock. It is said that here, in 1523, Lachlan Cattenach of Duart Castle left his wife Elisabeth naked to drown on the rising tide, because she did not bear him a son. Although assumed to have drowned, she was rescued by a passing boat, and confronted Lachlan some time later in Inverary. On the 10th September 1524 Lachlan was killed in Edinburgh by Campbell of Calder, one of Elisabeth's relatives.

The island of Lismore, as a platform from which to view the surrounding sea and landscape, is unequalled. On the mainland to the north are the mountains of Kingairloch, to the north-east Ben Nevis, to the east Port Appin, Loch Creran and Benderloch, and to the south and west the islands of the Firth of Lorn, and Mull – surely one of the most stunning settings in the west Highlands.

David Hutcheson memorial, Kerrera

The Caledonian MacBrayne vehicle ferry Eigg operates from Oban to Achnacroish, taking 50 minutes. A passenger ferry makes a much shorter crossing to the northern tip from Port Appin, where the ferryman lives.

Shuna Island, One-and-a-half miles northeast of Lismore, is owned by a Glasgow industrialist and run as a farm; to the south of the fine white farmhouse is the substantial ruin of Castle Shuna. To the north-east of Shuna is the small **Eilean Balnagowan**. At the entrance of Loch Creran is the island of **Eriska**, reached via a narrow bridge. The fine turreted Eriska House is now a luxurious hotel.

In Loch Laich, on the tidal isle of the falconer, stands the beautiful rectangular **Castle Stalker**, ancient seat of the Stewarts of Appin, built in the 15thC and used by James IV as a hunting lodge. It later fell into ruins, but has recently been restored. It is private.

Kerrera

Strathclyde. Four-and-a-half miles long by two miles wide, Kerrera lies to the west of Oban – a natural breakwater for one of the best harbours on the west coast of Scotland. The island is green and hilly, composed of a mixture of secondary basalt, graphitic schists and old red sandstone.

The island has belonged to the Mac Dougalls since the founding of the Clan by Somerled in the 12thC. In 1249 King Alexander II of Scotland, with his fleet, anchored in The Horse Shoe bay, determined to wrest the Hebrides from King Haakon of Norway, but Alexander died quite suddenly, his army dispersed and his body was taken to Melrose. His visit is commemorated in the name of the land behind the bay – *Dalrigh*, the field of the King. Later, in 1263, King Haakon rallied his fleet in the bay, en route to the Battle of Largs where he was defeated, and the remains of his force once again anchored off Kerrera before

travelling home to Norway. King Haakon never completed the journey, being taken ill and dying in Orkney.

Gylen Castle, the ruins of which now stand at the southern end of Kerrera, was built on the site of an earlier fortification in 1587 by Duncan MacDougall of Dunollie, the 16th Chief. The building, a handsomely detailed tower standing above the cliffs, was beseiged in 1647 by General Leslie during the Covenanting Wars and subsequently burned. It has never been restored.

Kerrera was used for many years as a stepping stone between Mull and the mainland. Cattle were swum to the mainland from Ardantrive Bay at the north-east tip of Kerrera, where there are a jetty and moorings. The prominent memorial at the north end above the bay commemorates David Hutcheson, one of the founders of what is now Caledonian MacBrayne.

By 1861 the population of the island was 105, in 1879 a post office was established, and the present schoolhouse and church overlooking the Sound of Kerrera, were built in 1872. The population is now about 50.

This compact and attractive island is ideal for gentle walks in attractive scenery, having fine views of Mull and Lismore to the west and north.

It is easily reached by the small passenger ferry which operates from Gallanach-beg, to the south of Oban.

Tiree and Coll

Tiree

Strathclyde. The north-east corner of Tiree is 15 miles from Treshnish Point, Mull, and is separated from its island partner, Coll, to the north-east, by the two-mile wide Gunna Sound. It lies as far west as Harris in the Outer Hebrides, and measures a little over ten miles long by about six miles at the widest point, with an area of 19,000 acres. It was called *Tir-Iodh* (the land of corn), and was once known as the granary of the isles for, although the bedrock is Archaean gneiss, a poor infertile rock, over two-thirds of it has been deeply covered with wind-blown shell sand, which has blessed the island with fertile, well-drained machair,

deep enough for the plough.

The landscape of Tiree is unique among the larger Hebridean islands, being one of houses and not hills. It is flat, for the most part a hairline on the horizon with only two high points: Ben Hynish in the south rising to 462 ft, and Ben Hough in the north-west rising to 390 ft. Average rainfall is low, about 45-50 inches, and there are more hours of sun in the spring than anywhere else in Scotland, with an average of 223 hours in May. But Tiree's fertile soil is brought by the wind, and there is no shelter from it – in February 1961 it gusted at 116 mph, a record at the time – and living on Tiree has been likened to living on the deck of an aircraft carrier.

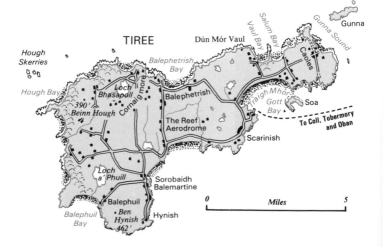

The population peaked at 4450 in 1831; 50 years later it was 2700, following the potato famines and forced evictions. In 1885 there was a revolt against the landowners, when landless families took over a vacated farm and demanded it be turned into crofts. The government sent two ships, the *Ajax* and the *Assistance*, and marines to deal with this disturbance; five men were arrested and imprisoned for a short while, but there was no fighting, and the marines became great friends with the islanders. With the passing of the Crofters' Act in 1886 (*see* Skye) the farms were split into the present 270 or so small crofts, maintaining a higher population (now 870) on the island than if amalgamated. Cattle and sheep are grazed on the fertile machair, and crops provide winter fodder. There is a lobster-fishing industry, which has benefited from the building of a pier at Caoles. Trawling ceased due to over exploitation.

Evidence of occupation on Tiree dates back to 800 BC – pottery and tools uncovered at Dùn Mór Vaul date from this period. A broch was built on the site of this earlier settlement. In AD 565 Batheine, a follower of St Columba, founded a monastery at Sorobaidh. St Columba also visited Tiree; in legend he cursed a rock in Gott Bay to remain weedless after his boat struck it and nearly sank.

The Vikings raided Tiree – they burnt Sorobaidh in AD 672 – then later settled; Norse burials have been found at Cornaigbeg. Control then passed to the Kingdom of Man and the Isles, and, in 1123, Reginald son of King Godfrey, ruled the area which included Tiree.

In 1164, upon the death of Somerled, his son Dougall inherited the island (along with Coll and Mull) which he in turn passed on to his son Duncan. After the defeat of the Norwegian force under King Haakon at the Battle of Largs in 1263, control of the isles passed to Alexander III of Scotland who confirmed ownership upon the MacDougalls. The Scottish Wars of Independence brought changes in ownership, with the MacDonalds acquiring Tiree (and Coll), only to return it to the MacDougalls in 1354. Their influence was negligible and, by 1390, Lachlan MacLean was Baillie of Tiree and Coll, his descendants disputing ownership until the 16thC. In 1562 and again in 1578, Tiree was invaded by the MacDonalds of Islay; in the latter part of the 17thC the present owners, the Argylls, took control.

The traditional homes on Tiree were of the black house type (*tigh dubh*), with drystone walls up to nine-feet thick, rounded corners and a thatched roof resting on inner walls – all designed so that the gales would sweep over them. These have now been converted into white houses (*tigh geal*) with cemented stones, tar and felt roofs and a fireplace at one end, and the outside painted white.

The main pier and ferry terminal, sheltered in most conditions, is in Gott Bay, to the west of the Tràigh Mhór which is a fine beach, the longest in Tiree. Scarinish, the main village behind the old harbour, has a post office, shops and hotel.

At Tiree's flat centre is The Reef, an airfield built by the RAF in 1941 on the site of a grass landing-strip, from where 518 Squadron flew Halifax and 218 Squadron flew Warwicks. With the airfield came good roads and electricity, and it is now used for civil aviation, with a regular daily service from Glasgow operated by Loganair. The weather station here, which reports regularly for the BBC shipping forecasts, is a legacy of the early work done by D. O. MacLean, Head of Cornaigmore School, who started keeping records in 1926.

To the south of Sorobaidh Bay is Balemartine, the largest village, with many *tigh geal*. At the end of the road to the south is Hynish, with granite houses built for the workers on the Skerryvore lighthouse. Standing ten miles south-west of here, it is 138 ft from the base to the lantern, on a rock only ten feet above mean high water and was built in 1838-43 by Alan Stevenson, another uncle of Robert Louis Stevenson, the 4308 tons of granite used in its construction being quarried on the Ross of Mull. First lit in 1844, it was extensively damaged by fire in 1954, following which new diesel generators were installed. The sea area between the rocks and reefs of the Skerryvore and Tiree can be extremely rough during north-westerly gales. Above the Hynish is a granite tower, once used to signal to the lighthouse.

The pretty white houses of Balephuil stand to the east of a mile of beach backed by flat machair, in the midst of which Loch a' Phuill glistens. Above the village is Ben Hynish, from the summit of which there is a fine view of Skerryvore. On the west coast there are extensive areas of dunes grazed by cattle and sheep, and behind these grow crops of barley and corn.

Off the north-west corner of Tiree there are numerous rocks and skerries. Behind the shell-sand bay of Cornaigmore is Loch Bhasapoll, surrounded by machair, and known for its duck population. On its north side it is said that there was once a township called Baile nan Craganach (the town of the clumsy ones); five men each with 12 fingers lived there. The next bay east, Balephetrish Bay, takes its name from *Baile Pheadairich* (the township of the storm petrel), and is where Tiree marble, pink flecked with green and quarried between 1791 and 1794 and again briefly in 1910. On the coast is Clacha Choire, the ringing stone, a glacial erratic which originated on Rum, said to contain a

Balephuil Bay, Tiree. *D Hardley*

crock of gold – but if it is ever split, Tiree will disappear beneath the waves. Such legends were collected by John Gregorson Campbell, minister of Tiree from 1861 to 1891, and published in his *Superstitions of the Scottish Highlands* in 1900.

On the rocky coast to the west of Vaul Bay is Dùn Mór Vaul (fort of the big wall), built in the 1stC. On the east of the island, at Caoles, there are attractive outcrops of pink orthogneiss. Across Gunna Sound lies the island of **Gunna**, once inhabited, now grazed by cattle.

Tiree can fairly lay claim to being the sunshine island, and in the spring and early summer the extensive machair lands are thick with blossom and heady with perfume. The island's large and robust population imparts a feeling of activity rare in the Western Isles.

The Caledonian MacBrayne vehicle ferry *Lord of the Isles* runs from Oban to Gott Bay – a four-and-a-quarter hour journey via Coll. It is the only ferry between these two islands. Loganair operate a daily flight (not Sundays) from Glasgow to The Reef airfield and on to Barra. There is a post bus service.

Coll

Strathclyde. With an area 18,300 acres, Coll measures thirteen-and-a-half by four miles, lying two miles north-east of Tiree and seven-and-a-half miles to the west of Caliach Point, Mull.

The northern two-thirds of the island are Lewisian gneiss, showing itself everywhere, its low hummocks infilled with peat bogs and lochans. The remaining

third of Coll, apart from the extreme south-west tip which is also gneiss, consists of very ancient metamorphosised sandstones containing quartz and marble, particularly beautiful by the shore at Gorton. The west coast has a covering of wind-blown shell sand, forming dunes over 100-ft high and machair suitable for grazing. The summit of Ben Hogh (341 ft) is the highest point; on its northern side are two glacial erratics, boulders of gabbro, probably from Mull. There are raised beaches at Arinagour and Arnabost.

The climate, like that of Tiree, is favourable, with many hours of sunshine early in the summer, mild winters and rainfall that is less than 50 inches each year. It is, of course, windy.

The early history of Coll is closely linked to that of Tiree – Norse settlement followed by the rule of Somerled and then Clan Donald. By 1841, the population had risen to 1440 and the laird, MacLean, given the island by Clan Donald, was unable to support such numbers and, during the next 15 or so years, half the population was cleared to Australia and Canada. In 1856 MacLean sold the island to the Stewarts, and now two-thirds are owned by a Dutch millionaire.

The shock waves of such a drastic solution as clearance continued for many years with further clearances and continued depopulation. The emphasis of agriculture turned to dairy cattle and the production of the famous Coll cheese, with farmers from Kintyre being brought to the island. With this came the virtual demise of Gaelic culture and language on Coll. At the turn of the century the market for dairy produce collapsed, and a gradual shift to stock-raising

Breachacha Castle, Coll. *D Hardley*

began. Today there are about 1000 beef cattle, a few dairy cattle, and 7000 sheep. The current population is about 140. There is a lobster-fishing industry, the numerous rocks and skerries off the north-east tip providing breeding grounds. At one time ling were caught and salted, but this industry died due to over-fishing.

Arinagour, Coll's only village lies on the west side of Loch Eatharna, and about half the population lives here. There are shops, a church, post office, hotel, school and bicycles for hire. The pier, built in 1967, is a stopping point for the Oban and Tiree

ferry. The coast to the north-east, and the land behind, is empty.

The road to Breachacha lies a little less than a mile inland from the south-east coast, which is deeply bayed and attractive. The

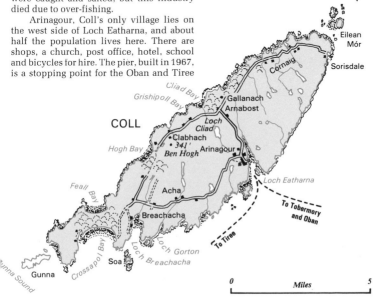

ancient Breachacha Castle, standing by the shore of the loch, was thought to have been the 14thC home of the MacLeans, part of the defences of the Lords of the Isles, but recent excavations now suggest 15thC construction. It is a good example of such a medieval fortress, little altered. It is now the headquarters of The Project Trust, run by Major Maclean-Bristol, which trains young volunteers for aid work overseas.

The newer castle close by was built in 1750 by Hector MacLean and visited by Boswell and Johnson on their tour of the Hebrides in October 1773, being entertained there by Coll's last hereditary piper. Confined to the building by a series of gales, they condemned it as a mere tradesman's box.

After a battle in 1593 between the MacLeans of Coll and the invading Duarts, the burn that flows into Loch Breachacha was choked with Duart heads, and ducks swam in the blood – it is now called *Struthan nan Ceann*, the stream of the heads.

To the west a neck of marram dunes separates Crossapol Bay from the very beautiful Feall Bay to the north. Two miles away, beyond Gunna, lies Tiree – close, but unreachable from here. The west coast is broken into sandy dune-backed bays by low rocky headlands, the valleys between these headlands sheltering the farms. The golden sands of Hogh Bay are fringed with rose- and ochre-coloured gneiss glistening with mica. The tiny Clabhach Bay has white sand, Grishipoll Bay is rocky, Cliad Bay has shell sand. At Arnabost the school, now in ruins, was built over an earth house where the islanders hid during Viking raids, the entrance was beneath the school porch.

The coast north of Gallanach Farm, Coll's largest, is one of pretty and secluded coves, the haunt of many seabirds. Cornaig was once the centre of the ling fisheries; it is now an area of prosperous farms intersected with trout streams, and off the north-east tip are rocks and skerries which are fished for lobster.

To the east a lonely dwelling is all that remains of the community of Sorisdale, and between here and Arinagour there is little but wet and rocky moorland, lochs and streams.

Coll is reached by the Caledonian MacBrayne ferry *Lord of the Isles* from Oban, which also provides the link with its green and populous neighbour, Tiree.

The islands of Nether Lorn

Seil

Strathclyde. A 'slate island', Seil has been joined to the mainland since 1792 by Robert Mylne's Clachan Bridge, upon which grows the fairy foxglove, *Erinus alpinus*. The ancient inn by the bridge was used by the Highlanders after the '45 rebellion to change from trousers into the forbidden kilt which could be legally worn only 'overseas'. The remains of disused slate workings which closed down in 1965, can be seen at Balvicar and at Easdale, where the sea flooded the quarries in November 1881, and overnight 240 men lost their livelihoods. The island is farmed, lobsters are fished, and there is now a population of 500.

The island of **Easdale**, with a popula-

Easdale, Seil

tion of about 30, reached by a small passenger ferry from Ellanbeich, has workers' cottages around a harbour. Most of these dwellings are now holiday homes, and the island, owned by an Englishman, is reminiscent of North Wales. There is an excellent folk museum. To the south-west is the tiny island of Belnahua, itself once a slate quarry, and to the west is the cliff-bound and grassy **Insh Island**, with caves at the northern end. In 1873 a herd of 192 pilot whales were left stranded by the tide in Clachan Sound which separates Seil from the mainland.

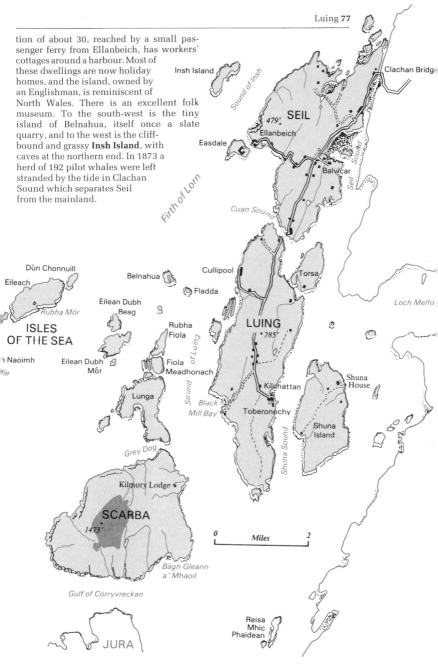

Luing

Strathclyde. Pronounced ling, this is, like Seil, a slate island. The main village is Cullipool on the west coast, where the quarries which closed down in 1965 once employed 150 men and produced 700,000 slates each year. Slates from here were used to re-roof Iona Cathedral. It is now a lobster-fishing centre, with the lobster pond at Fraoch Eilean being one of Scotland's largest. Luing is also well known for the prize beef cattle bred by the island's owner. The island's population is now 200. On a ridge to the south of Torsa are the remains of two Iron Age forts, Dun Ballycastle and Dun Leccamore, which has some rooms and a stairway remaining.

A road runs from the ferry at Cuan Sound to Toberonochy on the east coast. Above the village is the ruined chapel of Kilchattan, surrounded by some magnificent slate gravestones including that of the Covenanter Alex Campbell, who 'digged my grave before I died'. At the island's centre is a school, a new church, and a ruined water mill, with the Fairy Knoll not far away, a favourite resting place for travellers who should place a hair or thread on top to gain favour with the spirits of the glen. The view from the west side of the island's modest summit (285 ft), towards the Isles of the Sea and the Ross of Mull, is ample reward for the easy climb. To the east of Toberonochy lies **Shuna**, wooded and grazed by sheep, on which is the castellated Shuna House at the north-west corner. To the east of Cuan Sound is the green island of **Torsa**, reached from Luing at low tide, with a farmhouse in the south and the ruined 16thC fortress of Caisteal nan Con, Castle of the Dogs, once a hunting lodge of the Lords of the Isles. There was once a thriving crofting community on the island.

Luing is served by both passenger and vehicle ferries which operate from the south of Seil across the swift-flowing waters of Cuan Sound.

The Isles of the Sea

Strathclyde. These islands are commonly known as the Garvellachs, deriving from *Garbh Eileach* (rough isles). Lying about three miles west of Luing, their remoteness is made greater by the rocks and reefs of the surrounding seas. The north coasts comprise steep cliffs with sea caves, sloping to the more sheltered south sides, where landings can, with caution, be made.

Eileach an Naoimh (pronounced ellan nave) is the most southerly. It has some substantial remains of behive cells from the original monastery founded by St Brendan in AD 542, 21 years before Iona. Landings are made at Port Columcille, where there is a small shingle beach and a freshwater spring. Nearby are a ruined chapel and burial ground – a stone slab is supposed to mark the grave of Eithne, St Columba's mother, although this is unlikely. This island is thought to have been St Columba's secret retreat, as close to his heart as Iona; it was referred to as Hinba from the Gaelic *Na In Ba* (isle of the sea).

The small island of **A' Chùli** is reputed to have been St Brendan's resting place. Landings can also be made at Rubha Mór on **Garbh Eileach**, where there is a small burial ground. The northern-most island is **Dùn Chonnuill**, where the ruined 13thC castle is said to stand on the site of an earlier fortress build in the 1stC by Conal Cearnach, an Irish king. There are trips around the islands from Cuan on Luing.

Lunga

Strathclyde. Lunga (Isle of the Longships) is situated to the north of Scarba, separated by the Grey Dog tide-race. The grassy top of the island rises to a height of 321 ft and is grazed by sheep, and the northern extremity breaks into several smaller tidal islands; the most northerly, Rubha Fiola, is run as an adventure centre for young people, who stay in the timber chalet, by the remains of an old blackhouse. The graves of some of Lunga's past inhabitants can be found in the burial ground of Kilchattan on Luing. At the northern end of Lunga is St Columba's Well, which has never run dry and was used by quarry workers on Belnahua in time of drought.

To the west are the low-lying islands of **Eilean Dubh Beag** and **Eilean Dubh Mór**, beyond which rise the mysterious Isles of the Sea.

To the north are the tiny lighthouse island of **Fladda**, and **Belnahua**, one of the 'slate islands', with its deserted quarries and cottages, all grey and windswept. To the east is Luing, across the swift-flowing waters of the sound.

Scarba

Strathclyde. The name derives from the Norse *Skarpoe* (rough isle). Three miles long by two-and-a-half miles wide it lies to the north of Jura across the Corryvreckan tide-race, separated from Lunga, to the north, by another tide-race, the Grey Dog. Although it is grazed by cattle and sheep, the island is basically rough and craggy – graphite schist in the east, and quartzite in the west where it rises to a height of 1473 ft – and the coast is rocky, with many caves. At one time it supported 14 families.

On the east side, above woodland, is the refurbished Kilmory Lodge. Bàgh Cleanh a' Mhaoil in the south has a good beach, but further round to the west are the whirlpools of the Gulf of Corryvreckan. Above Port nan Urrachan, on the west coast, are the remains of early Christian behive cells.

Colonsay and Oronsay

Strathclyde. With a joint population of 130, these two islands, joined by sand passable at low tide, cover 11,075 acres, and are 10½ miles long by 3¾ miles wide, lying a little over eight miles to the west of Jura. They have been inhabited for 7000 years: neolithic flint tools and the bones of domesticated animals were found in Uamh Uir (the cave of the grave) on the south side of Kiloran Bay. In the dunes a Viking ship burial was uncovered, the warrior having been buried along with his weapons, horse and coins dated AD 831-854.

The name Colonsay probably derives from *Chaileiney* (Colin's Island). The land is lower mudstone strata of Torridonian sandstone containing lime, and breaks down into good soil. There are some basalt dykes, and much of the higher ground is broken moorland and scrub inhabited by shaggy wild goats. There are raised beaches on the west coast (fine examples are seen to the north of Kiloran Bay behind Port Sgibinis), evidence of a time when the sea level was higher, and Colonsay was in fact four islands. There are also beaches backed by machair on the west – the Tràigh Bàn, Kiloran, and Plaide Mhór are particularly notable. The valley by Rubh' a' Geodha in the north is dune-filled – a rabbit warren culminating in a beautiful beach facing east.

To the west of Kiloran village, the coast around Pig's Paradise (where pigs were once kept) is all craggy high cliffs cut by deep ravines – a superb place from which to view Mull, Iona, the Torran Rocks and Dubh Artach lighthouse. The highest point is Carnan Eoin (the hill of the birds), rising to 470 ft to the north-east of Kiloran Bay. The Piper's Cave, on the coast beneath Beinn Bhreac, is the cavern where, in legend, a piper went in search of hell. He was never seen again, but his dog appeared from another cave four miles south, with all his hair singed off.

The first known owners of Colonsay were the MacPhees, followed by the Campbells of Argyll, and in 1701 it was purchased by Malcolm McNeil of Knapdale. In legend the McNeils of Colonsay are descended from a family that, with their cattle, came across from Barra in an open boat. McNeil's wife gave birth on the trip, one of the beasts being slaughtered and the mother

and child placed inside the carcass for warmth and shelter. Malcolm McNeil built Colonsay House in 1722, using stones taken from Kiloran Abbey.

In the 19thC the McNeils planted many trees in Kiloran Valley, which provided shelter for the fine gardens developed by Lord Strathcona, who bought the islands in 1904, planting rhododendrons, azalea, eucalyptus, acacia, maple and magnolia. The woods have elm, ash, beech, sycamore, spruce, larch, silver fir and pine. Palm trees and bamboo grow in the open, sheltered by the gentle valley which creates a mild micro-climate. Lord Strathcona took a great interest in the island and its people, stemming depopulation and giving stable management that ensured long-term prosperity.

Colonsay House is now converted, for the most part, into holiday flats, and the gardens are a shadow of their former glory.

The economy of Colonsay is based on crofting and farming with a little fishing, supplemented by a limited amount of tourism. Milk and butter are produced for home consumption. There is a hotel, some summer cottages and bed-and-breakfast accommodation. For the peak holiday period, it all is usually fully booked.

The ferry terminal is at Scalasaig, the main village, where the pier was built in 1965. There is a post office/store, petrol pump and resident doctor here as well as the hotel. The other areas of population are Kilchattan in the west, and Kiloran. The island has its own junior school, and there is a minister, but no police. Gaelic is the predominant language.

To the east of the bays of Tobar Fuar (cold well) and Port Lobh (apparently Port Stink, from the rotting seaweed, but definitely not always so), there is a simple 18-hole golf course. The large central Loch Fada and many coastal locations provide excellent birdwatching, and there is much fine walking. Off the west coast of the grassy Ardskenish peninsula, there is a small colony of seals among the skerries.

The island of Oronsay is reached across The Strand, a wide expanse of dull shell sand which is dried out about three hours either side of low water – it is advisable, however, to seek local advice before making the crossing. Halfway, in the sand, can be found the sanctuary cross – a fugitive fleeing from Colonsay was rendered immune from punishment when he reached the cross, provided he remained on Oronsay for a year and a day.

The name Oronsay derives from that of St Oran, a disciple of St Columba, who came here from Ireland in AD 563 and founded a monastery. The present ruined Augustinian priory is thought to have been built on the same site in 1380. The buildings are very fine, rivalling those on Iona, although on Oronsay farm buildings are uncomfortably close. In the chapel there is a high altar, in which are kept human remains which have surfaced in the graveyard nearby. Outside stands a Celtic cross, 12 ft high and of considerable beauty, and in a roofed building alongside the chapel are slab-shaped tombstones, carved with knights and various other figures.

Oronsay Farm was built by the McNeils using stones taken from the priory.

The highest point is Beinn Oronsay (305 ft), from which there are excellent views. There are two good beaches on the west coast, and rocks and skerries to the south. On **Eilean nan Ron** (seal island) there was once a kelp-gatherer's cottage, and there is still a colony of grey seals.

The Colonsay community is well balanced, and the island appears well tended. Those who wish to find peace in beautiful and unspoiled surroundings should seriously consider a visit.

The Caledonian MacBrayne vehicle ferry *Isle of Mull* operates from Oban on Monday, Wednesday and Friday, with some additional Tuesday sailings in mid-summer. *Claymore* operates an additional seasonal service from Kennacraig via Port Askaig (Islay). There is a post bus.

Crofts at Kilchattan, Colonsay

Islay, Jura and Gigha

Islay

Strathclyde. Islay (pronounced i-la), the green isle, measures 25 miles north to south and 20 miles east to west, and has an area of 150,500 acres. It lies 14 miles west of Kintyre, and a mile southwest of its close neighbour, Jura.

The geology of Islay is quite complex and, as a consequence, the landscape is varied. The southern end of the Rinns of Islay peninsula is Archaean gneiss with patches of hornblende, typically rough treeless grassland with rock outcrops. The northern part of the Rinns, around the head of Loch Indaal to Bowmore, is calcareous Torridonian sandstone with deposits of good loam; this is the agricultural heart of the island. The Northern tip is Cambrian quartzite with belts of Dalradian limestone running through it, and from Port Askaig to the Mull of Oa (pronounced o) there is a strip of mica schist intersected with limestone. To the south-east of this is the mountainous belt of Dalradian quartzite – a continuation of the rocks of Jura also containing similarly barren sporting coasts. On the extreme southeast coast, between Port Ellen and Ardtalla, there is a fringe of mica schist and hornblende, giving a beautifully broken coastline of bays and islands, backed by areas of woodland and scrub.

Coasts exposed to the west have benefited from deposits of windblown shell and the machair grassland this promotes. There are also extensive deposits of peat, used both as domestic fuel and for preparing malt in the island's eight whisky distilleries. It is also worth noting that Islay has some mineral potential; indeed, lead and silver were mined in the 19thC to the west of Port Askaig, and copper and manganese are both known to be present.

The tidal range on the east coasts of Islay and Jura is less than anywhere else in the British Isles. The spring range rarely exceeds five feet and may be as little as two. At neap tides the sea level seems to remain constant for days. The climate of Islay is typically oceanic. There is little shelter from the weather, and Loch Indaal tends to funnel the prevailing winds right to the centre.

There are prehistoric remains scattered all over the island, and written records are available for Islay from an earlier time than any other Hebridean island. The Irish came in the 3rdC, and St Columba is said to have founded a chapel at Kilchiaran, on the west of the Rinns.

On two islets in Loch Finlaggan, to the south-west of Port Askaig, there once stood castles from which the Lord of the Isles ruled the Hebrides, but there is now little left to be seen, and the land is private. John, first Lord of the Isles, erected the beautiful 14thC Celtic cross in the churchyard at Kilchoman (the cell of Comman, long since vanished) in the west in memory of his second wife, Margaret. It is eight-feet high, slim and elegant. At the base is a wishing stone, to be turned by expectant mothers who wish to have a son; the hollow in which it rests has been worn deep. To the north-west the foundations of the summer palace of the Lord of the Isles have been discovered and it is said that the legendary Skye piping family, the McCrimmons, derived their art from the magic black chanter (part of a bagpipe) obtained on Islay.

The main industries are farming, distilling, tourism and fishing. There are about 500 farms, and nearly all the farmers are the tenants of large estates. Sheep and beef and dairy cattle are kept – a mellow cheese is produced from surplus milk at the Port Charlotte Creamery, established in 1939. Barley was once grown for the distillers, but this raw material is now imported. The island's modest fishing fleet takes mostly shellfish, processed on the island.

On Islay, and throughout the Highlands, whisky was once distilled illicitly. Legitimate distilling began about 180 years ago, with many distilleries being built on the sites of old stills. For a period there was no duty payable on whisky produced and consumed on Islay, and drunkenness was rife, the standard of husbandry went into a decline and the ministers complained. Until recently there were eight distilleries each employing about 20 people and producing a combined total of four million proof gallons each year, of which 75 per cent was exported. The remaining 25 per cent, consumed on the British home market, resulted in the Exchequer receiving almost £7000 duty each year for every man, woman and child on the island. Although two are currently out of production, the distilleries are: Ardbeg, established on a site used by smugglers in 1815, producing a malt mostly used in blends; Bowmore, established in 1799 and the oldest legal distillery on Islay, producing malt; Bruichladdich, established 1881, producing malt; Bunnahabhainn, established in 1881, used in blends; Caol Ila, established in 1846, mostly blended; Lagavulin, built in the early 19thC on the site of an illegal still, producing malt; Laphroaig, established in 1820, producing a strong peaty malt, also used to blend Islay Mist, a milder flavour; Port Ellen, established in 1825, closed 1930 and re-opened in 1965 – it also provides malt for some of the island's other distilleries.

The main village of Islay is Bowmore, near the head of Loch Indaal, with a population of about 900. It is dominated by the unusual round church of Kilarrow, built that way in 1769 by the Campbells of Shawfield so there would be no corners in which the devil could hide. A pleasant wide street of shops and bars leads downhill to the small harbour. Islay's administrative centre, Bowmore has a school for over 500 children, a police station, hospital, hotels and tourist office.

To the north, at the head of the loch, is Bridgend, where a private road to Islay House crosses the main road. There are woods, and the area is covered with flowers in the spring and summer – daffodil, bluebell, celandine, primrose and wild hyacinth. On a hill nearby stands a memorial to John F. Campbell, collector of Islay folklore.

The main road passes some pleasant beaches, a distillery and a small lighthouse before reaching Port Charlotte, a pretty village of neat pastel-painted houses, known as the Queen of the Rinns, where there is also a museum and a small pier.

At the exposed western tip of the Rinns of Islay are port Wemyss and Portnahaven, separated by a burn and sheltered by two islands, the larger of which, **Orsay**, has a ruined chapel and a lighthouse. The west coast of the Rinns is rocky with some fine sandy bays, namely Lossit, Machir and Saligo. To the north of Saligo there are dramatic steep cliffs, and behind the bay is Loch Gorm, with the stump of a ruined castle on an islet, the largest expanse of water on Islay, where every winter there are enormous numbers of geese – barnacle (as many as 8000), greylag and Greenland white-fronted.

To the west of Loch Gruinart the land undulates towards the sand and machair of Ardnave Point, with low-lying **Nave Island** off the tip. Many fine stone farmhouses around here have been allowed to fall into ruin. At the head of the long sandy Loch Gruinart, a bloody battle was fought on 5 August 1598 between Sir Lochlan Mor MacLean of Duart and Sir James MacDonald of Islay, owing to a dispute over the ownership of land. It is said that the MacDonalds of Islay won with the magical help of Du-sith, the black elf. The remains of Kilnave Chapel with its 8thC cross, lying on the shore of the loch· about two miles south of Ardnave Point, is where, after the battle, the MacDonalds burned to death 30 of the MacLeans

of Duart, mistakenly believing they had killed their leader, Sir James. To the south of Loch Gruinart are extensive deposits of peat.

The area to the north of Ballygrant (on the road to Port Askaig), where limestone is quarried, is a hilly wilderness, the haunt of sportsmen: there are herds of deer, many pheasants, and lochs well stocked with trout. On either side of Rubha a'Mhail, the northern-most tip of Islay, there are raised beaches.

Port Askaig is one of the terminals used by the Caledonian MacBrayne ferry from Kennacraig. A small landing craft-type ferry plies across the swift-flowing Sound of Islay to Jura. There are a few houses, a store, an attractive hotel (dating from the 16thC) and a lifeboat station, all overlooked by Dunlossit House. To the north are two distilleries, to the south the coat is rocky with small bays, a haven for sea birds and seals. There is no road until Ardtalla. The lighthouse at McArthur's Head marks the southern entrance to the Sound of Islay.

To the west of the trackless mountains of Islay is the six-mile shell-sand beach of Laggan, backed by dunes and machair, with a golf course at the southern end. To the south-east is Port Ellen, a simple workman-like village and Islay's other ferry terminal, the largest centre of population, built 100 years ago, with shops, a bank and hotels. To the west of Port Ellen, Kilnaughton Bay has a fine beach. The point of Carraig Fhada is guarded by a curious white light tower built in 1832 and dedicated to Lady Eleanor Campbell. The Oa peninsula, the most southerly part of Islay, has a rock and cliff coastline with many caves, once the scene of illicit distilling and smuggling. At the Mull of Oa, above sheer cliffs with views of Antrim and Rathlin Island, stands the American Memorial, built by the American Red Cross to commemorate U.S. servicemen lost when the *Tuscania* was torpedoed in February 1918 and the *Otranto* was wrecked in a gale in October 1918. Many bodies were washed ashore here.

To the east of Port Ellen the road heads north-east to Ardtalla, through one of the most attractive and interesting parts of the island, with white-painted and tidily kept distilleries of Laphroaig, Lagavulin and Ardbeg standing by the shore. To the south of Laphroaig is the small island of **Texa**, a rocky hump with a ruined chapel, a ruined cottage and two wells. Somerled anchored his fleet in Lagavulin Bay in the 12thC. To

Sar

Saligo Bay

Machir Bay

Kilchiaran Bay

Lossit Bay

RINNS

Portnah

Orsay

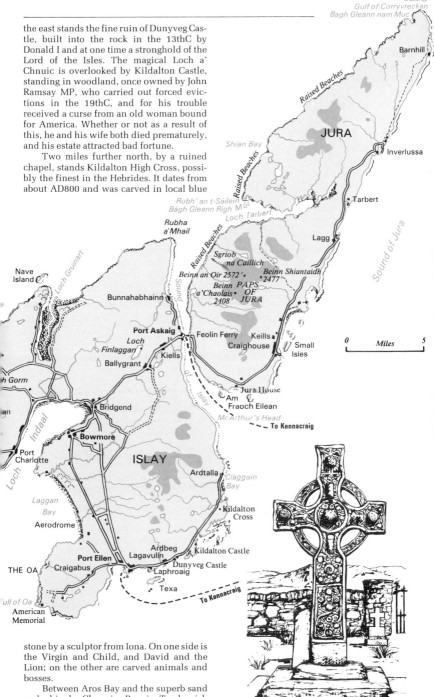

the east stands the fine ruin of Dunyveg Castle, built into the rock in the 13thC by Donald I and at one time a stronghold of the Lord of the Isles. The magical Loch a' Chnuic is overlooked by Kildalton Castle, standing in woodland, once owned by John Ramsay MP, who carried out forced evictions in the 19thC, and for his trouble received a curse from an old woman bound for America. Whether or not as a result of this, he and his wife both died prematurely, and his estate attracted bad fortune.

Two miles further north, by a ruined chapel, stands Kildalton High Cross, possibly the finest in the Hebrides. It dates from about AD800 and was carved in local blue

stone by a sculptor from Iona. On one side is the Virgin and Child, and David and the Lion; on the other are carved animals and bosses.

Between Aros Bay and the superb sand and shingle Claggain Bay is Trudernish Point, upon which stands a vitrified dùn (fort). Inland, and to the north-west of

Kildalton High Cross, Islay

The church of Kilarrow, Bowmore, Islay

Ardtalla, a scrubby woodland gives way to barren private sporting estates, where herds of deer roam and where there are many pheasants and lochs full of trout. With such a variety of habitat, and so much land left wild, it is not surprising that Islay has the richest bird life in the Hebrides, with over 180 different species having been recorded – an ornithologist's paradise.

Islay's population peaked at nearly 15,000 in 1831; it is now 4000. There are few job opportunities and many young men go to sea – Islay has been called a nursery of sea captains. Many of the farms have been taken over by Lowlanders and Gaelic culture has declined; although Gaelic is taught in the schools and spoken by the older folk, English still predominates. Islay has great agricultural potential, never fully realised, but Islaymen still believe that their island is the Queen of the Hebrides.

The island is served by the Caledonian MacBrayne vehicle ferry *Claymore* which operates from Kennacraig to Port Askaig and Port Ellen, and in summer links once a week with Oban and twice a week with Colonsay. Loganair fly to Islay from Glasgow. There is a bus service on Islay.

Jura

Strathclyde. Jura's name comes from the Norse *Dyr Öe* (deer island). It has an area of 93,700 acres (including Scarba), and is 28 miles long by eight miles wide, lying just half a mile from Islay. As well as a narrow strip of schist along the east coast, Jura has the largest area of metamorphic quartzite – a poor, infertile rock – in the Highlands.

Loch Tarbert almost bisects the island. In the southern half are the Paps of Jura, prominent landmarks for miles around: Beinn a'Chaolais (mountain of the sound) rises to 2408 ft, Beinn an Oir (mountain of the boundary, often called the mountain of gold) to 2572 ft, and Beinn Shiantaidh (holy mountain) to 2477 ft. The slopes are barren and scree-covered, but the views from the top are splendid – on a clear day Ireland and the Isle of Man are visible. To the north-west of Beinn an Oir is a large rock scar called Sgriob na Caillich, the witches scrape. The majority of the island is trackless blanket bog, with about 5000 red deer, some wild goats and, of course, birds. It is extemely difficult country to cross.

Along the west coast are raised beaches, long stretches of white stones among the grass and heather, formed when the sea level was higher. Notable are those at Bàgh Gleann Righ Mór, Rubh' an t-Sàilen and Shian. There are many caves, used for shelter by both the deer and their hunters, as sheep folds and, in the past, by the islanders transporting their dead to Iona and Oronsay. Rudimentary altars were built in some.

A large cave about 180 ft deep, at the northern end of Jura in Bàgh Gleann nam Muc, overloking the Gulf of Corryvreckan, is said to be the burial place of a Norwegian prince named Breacan, whose galley was consumed by the treacherous waters between here and Scarba. This tide-race runs west on the flood and east on the ebb at speeds of up to 10 knots (11.5 mph). A pinnacle of rock rising from the sea bed causes violent overfalls and breakers, with whirlpools on the Scarba side. Spring tides, and a westerly blowing against the flood, results in the maelstrom that can be heard many miles away. There is only a short period of slack water, when craft will pass through. The gulf is presided over by the legendary Caillich, an old woman who decides which ships shall sink and which shall survive, and indeed there have been some terrible disasters and some remarkable escapes. St Columba is said to have navigated it in full flood calming the waters with words alone.

The island of Jura was owned by the Clan Donald before being sold to the Campbells of Argyll in 1607, who later sold it in 1938. During the 18thC and early 19thC it was a centre for breeding Highland cattle, and the population rose to over 1300 in the

The Paps of Jura from Port Askaig

1840s. The glens were, at this time, green with grass. There then followed the widespread introduction of sheep, the despolitation of good land and mass emigration. Farming and crofting are now the main means of employment, with beef cattle and sheep being kept, but the major part of the island is used for sporting activities and is owned by five landlords.

All Jura's 250 inhabitants live on the east coast, and the main centre of population is at Craighouse, in the south of Small Isles Bay. There is a post office, shop, hotel, school, doctor and distillery – a new building, replacing the original built in the mid-19thC by the Campbells, which opened in 1963, with the product, a malt whisky, first being bottled in 1974. One of the two piers was buit in 1814 by Thomas Telford, and in Craighouse churchyard a stone commemorates Gillouir MacCrain, who saw 180 Christmasses before dying in 1645. To the north of Craighouse, Loch na Mile has a fine beach, and two-and-a-half miles offshore is the Skervuile Lighthouse. At the southern end of the island, Jura House stands among woods and rhododendrons. On the small island of **Am Fraoch Eilean** (heather isle), lying to the southwest, are the ruins of Caisteal Claidh (castle of the trench) built on the square Norman plan about 1154 by Somerled to defend the Sound of Islay.

Jura's only road finishes at Inverlussa,

passing through areas of moorland and patches of attractive woodland above the mainly rocky shoreline, although at Tarbert there is a fine sheltered beach.

Six miles to the south east is the remote **Eilean Mór**, the retreat of St Abban mac ui Charmaig (died AD 640) who founded a monastery at Keills on the mainland., On the island is a medieval chapel, once used as an ale house, built around an older building; it was visited by John Paul Jones during the American War of Independence. There is a standing cross close by, and a replica of another to the south on higher ground, and there is also a small sanctuary cave.

In the graveyard at Inverlussa lies Mary MacCrain, another member of a family noted for its longevity; she died in 1856, aged 126. A track continues towards the north of the island, passing close to Barnhill, the stone farmhouse where George Orwell wrote *Nineteen Eighty-Four*.

Jura stands in complete contrast to the fertile land of its well-endowed neighbour, Islay, but it is blessed with a sheltered position and a mild climate – palm trees and fuschias grow in the open.

It is unlikely that it will ever be much more than trackless moor and mountain, but its rugged beauty will continue to tempt vistors on to the small vehicle ferry which plies between Port Askaig and Feolin.

Gigha Island

Strathclyde. Gigha is pronounced gee-ah with a hard g. Although it has been suggested the name may derive from the Norse *Gjedöe* (goat island), a more apt and descriptive alternative is *Gud-ey* – good island or God's island – for what appears barren and rocky at a distance is a fertile and productive island with much good grazing (900 acres of arable land out of a total of 3600 acres) and a mild climate.

A ridge of epidiorite runs the length of Gigha, and the surrounding land is a lime-free sandy loam, which is best on the east. The highest point is 331 ft, at the summit of Creag Bhan, and there are some fine sandy beaches.

The island is divided into about a dozen farms and half a dozen crofts. A large stock of Ayrshires produce over 250,000 gallons of milk a year, and there are also some beef cattle and sheep, but no longer a commercial fishing industry.

The island was purchased in 1944 by the late Sir James Horlick (maker of the well-known beverage), who modernised the farms and converted 50 acres of woodland into the supremely beautiful and well-tended Achamore Gardens, transplanting many specimens from his garden near Ascot. Rare plants from Achamore are now being propagated and planted at Brodick, Arran. There are, among varied deciduous woodland, laburnum, *Primula candelabra*, azalea, hybrid rhododendron and various sub-tropical plants including palms and palm lilies *(Cordyline australis)*. The gardens were gifted to the National trust for Scotland in 1962 and are open during the summer.

The main area of population (which totals 190), the only village and the ferry terminal is Ardminish. Here there is a shop, post office (where bicycles can be hired) and an attractive hotel. The church has a stained-glass window dedicated to Kenneth MacLeod (born on Eigg in 1872), translator and composer of songs, including 'The Road to the Isles'. South of the village is the ancient chapel of Kilchattan, with an ogham stone nearby.

Over 70 species of birds have been recorded on Gigha; **Eun Eilean**, off the west coast, is noted for its sea birds and there is gullery on Eilean Garbh, to the north. None of the usual mammals exists on Gigha – deer, stoat, weasel, mole, fox and hare have never established themselves, and the rabbits were almost completely killed off by myxomatosis. Grey seals play off the rocky shores and around the numerous outlying reefs and skerries, and wild flowers bloom everywhere. The Gaelic-speaking community is well balanced with a high proportion of young people – testimony to the far-sight-

edness of Sir James Horlick. Gigha is a rare mixture of stability, viability and beauty. It should not be missed.

The Caledonian MacBrayne vehicle ferry *Bruernish* runs to the island from Tayinloan, Kintyre.

To the south of Gigha is barren **Cara Island** (from the Norse *Karoe*, coffin island), uninhabited for over 30 years. On it are an empty house and a ruined 15thC chapel; it is grazed by sheep and goats, and there are also otters.

Achamore House, Gigha

The Clyde islands

Bute

Strathclyde. Bute measures 16 miles by 4 miles, with an area of 31,000 acres. Its northern half is enclosed by the Cowal peninsula which seems, in places, only a stone's throw away across the Kyles of Bute. The Highland Boundary Fault splits the island along the line of Loch Fad – to the north is Dalradian schistose grit, to the south more recent old red sandstone with some basaltic lavas. To the north of Ettrick Bay the island is quite hilly, rising to 911 ft at the summit of Windy Hill.

Apart from the southern tip, the rest of the land undulates gently, and much is green and fertile. There are some areas of mixed woodland; Torr Wood, north of Kingarth, is particularly pleasant. As Bute is highly cultivated the bird life is not outstanding. The long-tailed field-mouse on the island is a sub-species of the mainland species with a shorter tail and smaller ears.

Prior to local council reorganisation in the early 1970's, Rothesay was capital of the County of Bute, which included Arran and the Cumbraes. Rothesay attained the status of a Royal Burgh in 1403, and the charter was extended by James VI of Scotland in 1584. The Bute family have for a long time taken an active interest in the affairs of the Burgh, often occupying the position of Provost. The history of the island is centred on the massive circular, moated Rothesay Castle, first recorded in 1230 when it was besieged by Norsemen, a portion of the eastern wall still showing signs of the breach made when they eventually captured the fortress, and in 1263 it fell to King Haakon of Norway. The wars of independence touched the castle little, although it was taken from the English by Sir Colin Campbell in about 1334. During the 15thC it was attacked by the Lord of the Isles.

During the reigns of James IV and James V it became an important base during their campaigns to subdue the Hebrides, a lawless part of the realm, and improvements were made to the fabric of the building, including the construction of the great tower, completed in 1541. In 1498 the Bute family were appointed hereditary keepers of the castle (an office still held by the present Marquess, although the Department of the Environment now maintains the building). The castle was successfully defended in 1527 against the rebel Master of Ruthven; however, the surrounding burgh was destroyed, a common occurrence each time

the castle was attacked and a hindrance to the continuing development of the town. In 1544 the Earl of Lennox took it for the English. When Cromwell withdrew his garrison in 1659 much of the building was dismantled; what was left was burned during the Duke of Monmouth's rebellion in 1685. The second Marquess of Bute began restoration in 1816, and further work was done by the third Marquess in 1872 and 1900.

Inside the massive sandstone curtain walls stands the chapel of St Michael; to the north-east of this is a well. The great hall, renovated in 1970 by the sixth Marquess, has a fine fireplace along one side, and a tapestry of the Prayer for Victory at Prestonpans on the wall. The castle is open to the public daily, and is well worth visiting, as is the museum to the south. At the top of the High Street is the ancient chapel of St Mary's, once part of the Bishopric of (the Isle of) Man.

Rothesay's population accounts for three-quarters of the island's total of 8100. It is a pleasant holiday place with a fine winter-garden and all the facilities a million visitors each year would expect, including visits from the *Waverley*, the last sea-going paddle steamer on the Clyde.

In 1882 the Rothesay Tramways Company began a horse-drawn tram service between Guildford Square in Rothesay and Port Bannatyne, and, after considerable suc-

0   Miles   5

cess, the line was electrified in 1902 and
extended to Ettrick Bay in 1905. The Company's eventual demise began with competition from motor coaches in the 1920s, and it
eventually became a summer-only service
in 1931 before the last tram ran on 30 September 1936. It was unique in being the only
such service on a Scottish island, comparable with that which still exists on the Isle of
Man.

Rothesay harbour, an important ferry
terminal, was built during the 17thC for the
fishing fleet, and subsequently rebuilt and
enlarged during the heyday of the Clyde
steamers. From 1940 to 1957 the bay was a
naval anchorage.

Prior to the advent of tourism as the
main industry Bute was a major supplier of
agricultural produce to the surrounding
mainland, and it is still very productive,
concentrating on dairy farming. The first
cotton mill was built in Rothesay in 1779
and this industry flourished in the early
19thC. Along with the rest of the west coast
of Scotland, there was a great deal of prosperity during the herring-fishing boom. Present industries, as well as tourism and
agriculture include weaving and shellfish
processing.

To the south of the capital is Kerrycroy
Bay, with very pretty houses among tall
trees at the back of a green, a sand and peb-
ble beach and a small stone jetty.
Mountstuart, to the south, has been the
home of successive earls and marquesses of
Bute for over 250 years. At Kilchattan, red
sandstone houses match the sand and
stones of the beach, and a track from the end
of the road leads to the lighthouse at
Rubha'n Eun, with fine views of the Cumbraes.

The southern tip of Bute is marked by
the steep St Blane's Hill, rising to 403 ft
above a rocky shoreline. A path from the
road's end leads to St Blane's Chapel, among
the ruins of a 6thC Celtic monastery in a
beautiful and secluded wooded glade.
Established by St Catan, the monastery took
the name of his nephew, St Blane. Remains
of the cells are still visible, and the chapel
shows fine 12thC craftsmanship. Dunagoil,
a vitrified Iron Age fort, stands on a promontory nearby.

The west-coast bays of Scalpsie, St
Ninian's and Ettrick all have sand, if only at
low tide. The low-lying island of **Inchmar-
nock** (675 acres) lie three-quarters of a mile
west of St Ninian's Point and chapel. It is
divided into two farms with two
farmhouses, and was recently offered
for sale for £250,000. Remains of the
monastery founded by St Marnoc in the
7thC can be seen, and cross fragments have
been uncovered around the ancient chapel.
A Bronze Age cairn containing three burial
cists has been excavated; in one was the

Kerrycroy, Bute

skeleton of a young woman and a fine lignite
collar. Except for a short period during
World War II when it was used for com-
mando training, the island has remained a
haven of peace, with prolific bird life
including the largest herring-gull colony on
the Clyde.

The main road skirts the low land
behind Ettrick Bay. At St Colmac, near the
chapel, is the Cross of Kilmachalmaig, possibly an old preaching cross. To the north-
west of the bay, the road ends at Clate Point;
inland, the hills are empty and unpopulated. At the north-west corner are the
remains of Kilmichael Chapel, destroyed by
the Norsemen, and higher up the hillside is
the burial cairn of Glenroidean.

Port Bannatyne is a northerly extension
of Rothesay. Kames Bay has a little sand, but
beyond this the shore is stony. The road
ends at Rhubodach, where a vehicle ferry
across the Kyles to Colintraive was established in 1950. The **Burnt Islands** to the
north are a natural haven for birds.

Bute is easily reached by the
Caledonian MacBrayne vehicle ferries *Juno,
Jupiter* and *Saturn* sailing between Wemyss
Bay and Rothesay (half hour crossing) and
by the smaller ferry *Loch Riddon* between
Colintrave and Rhubodach (five minute
crossing). There is a bus service on the
island, and the Tourist Information Centre
is in Rothesay.

The Cumbraes

Strathclyde. Great Cumbrae, part of the Bute
Estate, lies one mile west of Largs and just
over two miles east of Bute. Little Cumbrae
is half a mile to the south across The Tan;
between Rubha'n Eun on Bute and Little
Cumbrae passes all the Clyde shipping.

Great Cumbrae Island measures just
four miles by two miles, has an area of 5120
acres and attains a maximum height of 416
ft, the summit of the ridge of hills being
marked by the Glaid Stone. The coast is

Millport, Great Cumbrae

rocky and broken, with low cliffs. Central and northern areas are old red sandstone, with carboniferous limestone around Millport, and there are many igneous dykes, the outcrop known as The Lion on the south-east coast being particularly notable.

Millport wraps itself around the back of the bay, facing south towards Ailsa Craig and giving a spectacular view of Arran to the south-west. It offers all you would expect of a small resort, including golf, bowling, riding, boating, sea fishing, a cinema and an attractive museum of local history and has sandy beaches and pleasant gardens. A popular way of seeing the island is to cycle its 12-mile circumference, and bicycles can be hired in the town. The total population is about 1200.

During the late 19thC and early 20thC, the harbour was a regular port of call for the many Clyde steamers. In 1906 the steamer companies who objected to excessive pier dues, refused to call during the holiday season, and Great Cumbrae became a deserted island until Lloyd George arranged a compromise, just before the annual Glasgow holidays. The Episcopal church was consecrated as the Cathedral of Argyll and the Isles in 1876, and is the smallest cathedral in Britain. It was in Millport Bay in 1812 that Dr MacDougal first identified the roseate tern (Sterna dougalii) as a separate species.

The University Marine Biological Station is situated to the east of the town of Keppel pier. The rich marine life around the islands has been studied since the 1840s, when David Robertson, the Cumbrae Naturalist, made frequent visits, eventually establishing a floating laboratory in Kames Bay. The present buildings date from 1896, and were the headquarters of the Scottish Marine Biological Association until 1970

when it was transferred to Dunstaffnage, near Oban. The station is now controlled by the Universities of London and Glasgow. There are two research vessels and diving facilities, including a decompression chamber. Undergraduate and post-graduate courses are run, and independent research projects can be accommodated. For visitors there are an interesting aquarium and the Robertson Museum to be seen.

Close to the ferry terminal on the east side is the Scottish Sports Council's National Water Sports Training Centre, where sailing, sub-aqua and canoeing are taught. At the north-east tip – Tormont End – there are thought to be graves of Norsemen killed at the Battle of Largs in 1263. The rocky west coast is punctuated by the pleasant sand and shingle crescent of Fintray Bay.

Kirkton, in the south-west, was the first village on Great Cumbrae. There has been a chapel there since at least the 13thC – the present church dates from 1802. The inner road traverses the island's back-bone, and the views of Bute, Arran and the mainland are superb.

Little Cumbrae Island has an area of 700 acres and is privately owned, topped, at the western tip, by a disused lighthouse (the first light signal was built here in 1750). The house and farm buildings on the east, used as a holiday retreat, look over the remains of a tower on **Castle Island**. The Hunters of Hunterston were the castle's hereditary keepers until 1515, and in 1653 it was sacked by Cromwell. In the 14thC, Robert II and Robert III maintained the island as a deer forest. In 1845 Little Cumbrae supported four families, and over 5000 rabbits were taken each year.

In 1880 John Blain, a local historian, wrote: The islands of Larger and Lesser Cumbray intervene between Bute and the Continent. A local minister, thought to have been the Rev James Adam (1748-1831), also considered the islands of not little importance, praying for the inhabitants of Cumbrae and *the adjacent islands of Great Britain and Ireland.*

Caledonian MacBrayne operate the vehicle ferries *Loch Linnhe* and *Loch Striven* from Largs to Cumbrae Slip (10 minute crossing), where buses connect with Millport. There is a Tourist Information Centre in Largs.

Island of Arran

Strathclyde. The Island of Arran covers 105,600 acres, and is 20 miles long by 11 miles wide, lying three miles east of Kintyre in the Firth of Clyde. The name means 'high island'.

Arran was described by Sir Archibald Geike, the eminent geologist, as a complete synopsis of Scottish geology. James Hutton, the 18thC geologist, confirmed his theories of igneous geology on the island, and today Arran is visited regularly by scores of students who come to study the various rock formations. The island's most striking feature is the high peaks and corries of Goat Fell (2867 ft), an igneous intrusion into the surrounding Devonian sandstones and schists. This has resulted in a ring of upturned strata around the granite.

The south of Arran is new red sandstone, and in the north-east there is an area of carboniferous limestone. Throughout there are basaltic dykes which form ridges where the surrounding rock is softer (in the south) and fissures where the surrounding rock is harder (in the granite). Ice Age glaciers deposited many erratics and spread boulders of northern granite all over the south. A raised beach at the 25 ft level is easily recognised, virtually encircling the island.

Climate is mild Atlantic, with the low hills of Kintyre providing little shelter. Average rainfall varies from 50 inches in the west to 100 inches in the mountains, with the east receiving 70 inches. Snow generally lies only on the mountains, and frosts are rarely severe, and palm lilies, a sub-tropical native of New Zealand, grow in the open in the south and west.

Beef and dairy cattle and blackface and Cheviot sheep are kept, and potatoes are grown. Amazingly a special type of sand found on the island is exported to the Arab countries, but the main industry is tourism.

Brodick Castle, Arran

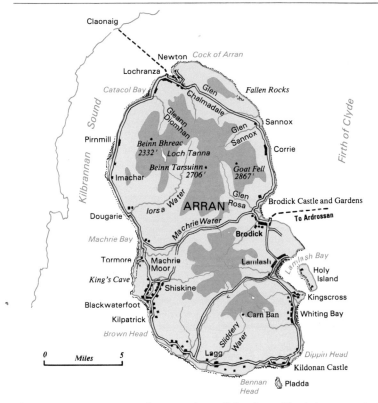

There is plenty of accommodation, and much to see and do in a relatively small area.

The history of Arran has much in common with the Hebrides. There are cairns, standing stones are to be found all around the coast and in the glens, and Bronze Age cists (burial chambers) have been found inside a stone circle on Machrie Moor. By 200 BC the Celtic people had arrived. Kilpatrick is thought by some to be one of the earliest Celtic Christian sites in Scotland, visite d in AD 545 by St Brendan; it was probably sacked by the Vikings in 797. St Mo Las (born AD 566) came to nearby Holy Island during the 7thC; it was later called Eilean Molaise after him, then becoming Lamlash, its name until 1830 and now the name of the village on Arran facing Holy Island.

Viking raids were followed by settlement. The Norsemen separated the island from the kingdom of Dalriada and held it until Somerled took it in 1156. After the Battle of Largs in 1263 the islands became part of the Kingdom of Scotland, under the Lord of the Isles.

In 1503 the island was awarded to the Hamiltons by Royal Charter. The Jacobite rebellion of 1745 hardly touched Arran at all, but the Highland clearances which followed caused massive emigration and the desertion of villages and crofts. The introduction of large-scale sheep farming which brought quick profits to the landlords eventually laid waste large areas. As land was enclosed for sheep, the people moved to small coastal holdings; when these were exhausted, they left for the industrial centres of the New World. Gaelic life and culture on Arran suffered a blow from which it was never to recover. Between 1821 and 1881 the population fell from 6600 to 4750; it currently stands at 3450. Arran is now owned by the family of the Duchess of Montrose, jointly with the National Trust for Scotland, and the Forestry Commission who hold between them 22,500 acres.

There are at present about 2000 red deer roaming wild, but at the end of the 18thC the herds had been hunted almost to extinction. Wild goats, once common, are now found only on Holy Island. There are no foxes, grey squirrels, stoats, weasels or moles, badgers are rare and adders are no longer as common as they were. All characteristic moorland birds are represented, and golden eagles are seen in the high peaks.

Most types of deciduous trees are present and there are two protected species unique to the island, rare whitebeams –*Sorbus arranensis* and *Sorbus pseudo-fennica*. Among the expected species of plants to be seen are some less common varieties – alpine lady's mantle grows in Glen Sannox, and alpine enchanter's-nightshade is sometimes found in areas of deep shade.

The great majority of Arran's thousands of visitors arrive at Brodick which has all main services and a new Tourist Information office near the pier. The village is unremarkable but its central position makes it an ideal touring centre. To the north of the bay is Brodick Castle and grounds, with Goat Fell behind, the summit of which can be reached after a pleasurable stiff walk. The castle and the mountain are both owned by the National Trust for Scotland. Although part of the castle, the Round tower, dates from the early 15thC, the vast majority owes its existence to the Hamiltons, who began building on to the earlier structure in 1558. In 1652 Cromwell's forces (later massacred by the islanders at Corrie) built the Battery and an additional wing. The final additions, including the Great West Tower, were started in 1844 by the architect Gillespie Graham, who was commissioned by William, son of the tenth Duke and his new wife, Princess Mary of Baden, a great-niece of the Empress Josephine. When the direct line of the Hamiltons finished in 1895 Brodick passed to the Duchess of Montrose.

The castle has an elegant simplicity, a fine example of the indigenous Scottish baronial style which belies the richness of its interiors. The drawing room is furnished with Italian marquetry and French gilt and ormolu pieces, and has a rich plaster ceiling. Other rooms contain Hamilton treasures, paintings by Watteau and Turner, and the Hamilton collection of sporting pictures, including works by Rowlandson, Pollard and Reinagle. The Victorian kitchen has been restored. The informal woodland garden of 60 acres, rich with rhododendrons, was started in 1923; the walled garden dates from 1710, now containing an area devoted to specimens from the late Sir James Horlick's garden at Achamore, Gigha. Brodick Castle and gardens are open from Easter until late September.

The Isle of Arran Heritage Museum is to be found at Rosaburn, housed in what was once an 18thC croft farm, with a smiddy, coach house, cottage, stables and bothy. There is also an excellent tea room, and garden, and demonstrations of lace making, spinning and weaving are given.

To the north of Brodick is Corrie, a village of gaily painted cottages around two tiny harbours. Stone used in the construction of the Crinan Canal was quarried in the hills behind. The road follows the coast to Sannox Bay, then turns north-west through North Glen Sannox and Glen Chalmadale to Lochranza. At the mouth of Glen Sannox are the remains of the old barytes mines, last worked in 1938, and there is a fine walk up the Glen beneath Cir Mhór on up to the high peaks.

At the northern end of Arran is an area of wild moorland, the haunt of red deer, and a dramatic stretch of coastline, with great rockfalls dating from the mesozoic and palaozoic periods. The large sandstone outcrop at the northern-most point is the Cock of Arran.

Lochranza is Arran's other ferry terminal, connecting with Claonaig, Kintyre. The village and youth hostel sit comfortably to the south of the loch, dominated by the ruined tower of Lochranza Castle, standing on a shingle spit. The existing building dates from the 16thC, with fragments of an earlier fortification, first recorded by Fordun in the late 14thC. In the early 15thC it was held by John de Mentieth; by 1450 it had been granted to Alexander Lord Montgomery by James II of Scotland. A key is available for those who wish to enter. The village was once a herring port, the anchorage well sheltered by the enveloping hills.

The west coast offers fine views of Kintyre across Kilbrannan Sound, and the shoreline is also extremely attractive – bright pebbles with the occasional sandy beach. At Catacol (from the Norse for ravine of the wild cat) are the Twelve Apostles, a pretty terrace of almost identical cottages overlooking the bay at the mouth of a steep-sided glen. At the summit of Glen Catacol, beneath the wild hills around Beinn Bhreac (2332 ft), is Loch Tanna, the largest loch on the island. On the coast to the west of the mountains is Pirnmill, where pirns (bobbins) were once made; there is a fine beach here. Past the palms of Whitefarland and Imachar, Iorsa Water empties into the sea by Dougarie Lodge, built by the Hamiltons and where Arran's first telephone was installed in 1891. The terraces of glacial material below the lodge are of great geological interest. Iorsa and Machrie Waters both contain salmon and trout, the island's most expensive fishing.

At Machrie Moor the hills retreat and evidence of the distant past is profuse. A stone circle above the road at Auchagallon, standing stones and circles on the moor, and remains of burial chambers, can all be clearly seen. A large cairn at Blackwaterfoot, spoiled during the 19thC, contained relics, including a dagger, which suggest a connection with the culture of southern England that conceived Stonehenge. From Tormore there is a fine walk above the stony shore to the King's Caves, eroded into the sandstone on the level of the 25-ft raised beach, on the walls of which early Christian or Viking carvings can be discerned. Traditionally the

Whitefarland, Arran, where palm lilies grow in the open

caves are associated with Robert Bruce, who came to Arran to try to oust the English, but it is unlikely that Bruce ever stayed in any of them. In the 18thC the Kirk Session met there, and in the 19thC they were used as a school. In legend they were occupied by Fingal, Fionn MacCaul.

The village of Shiskine, on the south of Machrie Moor, is said to be the burial place of St Mo Las. The String, the road across the island to Brodick, was built by Thomas Telford in 1817, passing through bare moorland and rough grazing.

The village of Blackwaterfoot stands in the centre of Drumadoon Bay, around a minuscule harbour. Towards the south the scenery becomes gentler and more pastoral, and a minor road follows Sliddery Water through the green glen to Lamlash. At Lagg, a supposedly haunted inn stands among trees by Kilmory Water, and at Torrylin the creamery produces Arran cheese. The rocky coast, once the haunt of smugglers from Ireland, lies a short walk to the south.

Three miles north-east of Lagg, in the valley of Allt an t-Sluice, a tributary of Kilmory Water, is Carn Ban, 950 ft above sea level. This chambered cairn, 100-ft long by 60-ft wide, dates from the neolithic period and has been little disturbed.

Kildonan overlooks the low-lying lighthouse island of **Pladda**, beyond which the triangular lump of Ailsa Craig looks deceptively close; to the south-west the Mull of Kintyre can be seen. There are some good areas of sand below the remains of Kildonan Castle, a mysterious 14thC ruin.

At Dippin Head the road rises high above the basaltic rocks of the shoreline, then descends to Whiting Bay, a sprawling village of cafés and craft shops, with a mainly stony beach. A mile up Glenashdale Burn, which enters the sea by the youth hostel, there are dramatic waterfalls, tumbling 100 ft down a lava sill, and to the north-east are the remains of a fort. A track leads from the village of Kingscross to Kingscross Point, where there are the substantial remains of a Viking fort and burial mound.

Lamlash is a sea-angling and sailing centre, spread along the north-east shore of Lamlash Bay facing towards Holy Island. The line of houses, hotels and shops are backed by trees and high moor, and by the beach there is a green. It is a delightful, relaxing place, where the hospital, council offices and high school are intermingled with craft shops and cafés. The large mooring buoys in the bay remain from the time when this was a fleet anchorage. In 1263 King Haakon moored here, en route to the Battle of Largs.

In summer there are boat trips across the bay to the nature reserve of **Holy Island**, a brooding hump rising to 1030 ft at the summit of Mullach Mòr. Above this island's small pier is the farmhouse, once again a family home, occupied by the island's new owners. There is a story that a farmer murdered his wife here, driven to it by her bearing him 15 daughters; she is supposedly buried under the kitchen floor. On the west side is the cave used by St Mo Las in the 7thC, with early Christian and Viking carvings on the walls. Below, near the shore, is the Judgement Stone, a flat sandstone table, and St Mo Las Well is nearby. Beyond the cave, at the south-west tip, is the larger of the island's two lighthouses. There are traces of a 12thC fortress built by Somerled, and in the early 14thC a monastery was established; the remaining small chapel was used for burials on Holy Island until 1790. The seaward side falls steeply to the sea, and a small lighthouse marks the south-east coast. Eriskay ponies, Soay sheep, Highland cattle and Saanen goats roam free, while on the rocky cliffs peregrines breed.

The major Caledonian MacBrayne vehicle ferry *Isle of Arran* operates from Ardrossan to Brodick, a 55 minute crossing. The smaller ferry *Loch Ranza* provides a seasonal service between Claonaig (Kintyre) and Lochranza, taking 30 minutes. There is a bus service on Arran, and cars and bicycles can be easily hired. The main Tourist Information Centre is in Brodick, with a smaller seasonal office at Lochranza.

Ardrossan is the ferry terminal for Arran. The tiny low-lying **Horse Isle** just outside the harbour is a refuge for five species of gull. **Lady Isle**, three miles south-west of Troon, is a natural haven for sea birds, with colonies of common, arctic and sandwich terns nesting. Roseate terns have also been seen, their numbers fluctuating from year to year.

Ailsa Craig

Strathclyde. This is a volcanic hump in the Firth of Clyde, ten miles west of Girvan and inhabited only by lighthouse keepers. It is two miles in circumference, and rises to a height of 1114 ft. In Gaelic its name means fairy rock and it is affectionately known as Paddy's Milestone. It has been mentioned in poems by both Keats and Wordsworth. It is composed of microgranite, acid igneous rock with fine-grained crystals of quartz, felspar and mica, and was quarried until quite recently. The quarrymen's cottages and the old trans-shipment pier, to the north, remain. The granite is famous for its use in the manufacture of curling stones.

Landings are made around high tide at the jetty by the lighthouse at Foreland Point in the north-east, and a narrow gauge tramway runs from here to the quarry. Other man-made relics include a forge, disused foghorns and the castle, a square tower about 300 ft up the slope behind the lighthouse. The building has little history, but it is said to have been used by the monks of Crossraguel Abbey near Maybole in Strathclyde, and was once held by Catholics on behalf of Philip II of Spain. Halfway up the eastern side of the hill there is a lochan, and from the top the view takes in the hills from Renfrewshire to Galloway, and Kintyre, Jura, Arran, Cowal, the Isle of Man and Ireland.

In the south-west corner is the Water Cave, approachable at low tide when it is also possible to walk right round the base of the island. There has been a colony of gannets on Ailsa Craig since at least 1526; between 1971 and 1974 their numbers were estimated at 9500 breeding pairs (about five per cent of the world gannet population), seen mainly on the southern side.

Boat trips are run from Girvan, weather permitting.

Sanda Island

Two miles off the south-east tip of Kintyre, this is a group of islands and skerries, including the small Sheep Island. Sanda consists of old red sandstone rising to a height of 405 ft, and was farmed until 1946. On it are the remains of the Bloody Castle and a chapel dedicated to St Ninian. It was much visited by the Vikings; in the burial ground is an old Norse grave. On the most southerly point is a lighthouse. **Sheep Island** and the tiny **Glunimore Island** are the most important breeding stations in the Clyde area for puffin.

In 1946 the lifeboatmen of Campbeltown made a remarkable rescue off Sanda, using the reserve boat *The Duke of Connaught*. Over a period of 18 hours, in terrible conditions, 54 passengers and crew and a dog were rescued from the 7000-ton *Byron Darnton*. The lifeboat pulled clear as the ship broke in two and, despite suffering engine trouble, returned safely.

Island Davaar

Sheltering Campbeltown Loch, this tidal island is linked to the mainland by a shingle causeway, treacherous when covered by the tide. On the northern tip of the island is a lighthouse, and on the southern side, in the fifth of the seven caves, is a wall painting of Christ crucified, executed in secret in 1887 by local artist Alexander MacKinnon, which caused a sensation when first discovered. MacKinnon was 33 when he painted the picture – he returned in 1934, aged 80, to retouch it. It is now a tourist attraction.

Index of islands